FROM THE
BATTLEFIELD TO THE
WHITE HOUSE
TO THE BOARDROOM

Leading Organizations
to Values-Based Results

D0808944

PRAISE FOR FROM THE BATTLEFIELD TO THE WHITE HOUSE TO THE BOARDROOM

"Bo masterfully applies his servant-leadership style through a shared vision and the development/empowerment of subordinates to establish an organizational culture of growth, inclusion, and the pursuit of excellence. Bo's ability to develop and seamlessly integrate an effective HR/People strategy into the long-term strategic objectives of an organization is truly remarkable. His innate emotional intelligence coupled with his intellectual capacity will transform any ineffective bureaucracy into a unified organization."

Colonel Luis A. Parilli, U.S. Army

"Bo is not much of a self-promoter, an attribute of a Servant Leader. But if you take the time to get to know Bo, ask next-level deep questions about his experiences, and discuss thoughts on leadership and management, you'd learn so much. You'd learn leadership through respect of others, and what it's like to mobilize thousands for military combat. You'd learn simple management tools to "get it done," and how to ensure the President of the United States is ready for his first interview as President when you hand him the phone. You'd learn leadership through participation and active engagement, and the art of execution through leading and managing a team. These are things I have learned from Bo through 20+ years."

Brent Westhoven, President, Mid-Atlantic, Advantia Health

"I have had the privilege of being mentored by Robert Brabo in one of the highest positions in the military. His accolades only paint a small picture of how great a leader and person he is. I am excited that others will now have the opportunity to learn from him, as I have. I have no doubt that his book will not only educate but inspire you! A must read!"

Mr. Bernard Simmons, Chief Warrant Officer Two, 82nd Airborne Division, U.S. Army

"I worked with Bo for several years at the White House Communications Agency — during my time in Joint Operations and as a Presidential Communications Officer (PCO). Bo was a consummate professional, the epitome of a leader. I could always walk into his office and get a straight, honest answer to every question or situation I presented to him. In addition, he would never say 'No.' His reply would always be 'This is how you do it.' And his answers were always on the money. In addition, Bo worked for me on several Presidential trips and I loved having him as one of my leads. I never had any concerns with his event sites. His team would always deliver 'Presidential' results and quality in a highly demanding and zero-defect environment. More than that, Soldiers/Sailors/Airmen/Marines loved working for Bo. He constantly demonstrated consistent qualities of a leadership at all times. I would love to work with him again!"

Lieutenant Colonel Chris Roth, U.S. Army (Retired), Communications and Technology Leader

FROM THE
BATTLEFIELD TO THE
WHITE HOUSE
TO THE *BOARDROOM*

Leading Organizations
to Values-Based Results

ROBERT "BO" BRABO

Foreword by Mike Barger, JetBlue Airways Co-Founder
and Former Navy TOPGUN Pilot & Instructor

SILVER TREE
PUBLISHING

DEDICATION

This book is dedicated to my fellow brothers and sisters in arms, who served the people of the United States and fought for our nation's freedom and the freedom of others. You fought so that future generations could live in as much peace as possible, so we all could have the ability to pursue our dreams and live without fear of persecution. To the American Soldiers, Sailors, Airmen, and Marines, you are the best of the best, and I am forever grateful to have served alongside you.

TABLE OF CONTENTS

FOREWORD

By Professor Michael Barger, Ed.D.

*Executive Director, Strategy and Academic Innovation, Stephen M. Ross
School of Business, University of Michigan; Former Chief Instructor, U.S. Navy
Fighter Weapons School (TOPGUN); Co-founder, JetBlue Airways*

As a Professor at the University of Michigan's Stephen M. Ross School
of Business, I have the privilege of teaching a unique and wildly
popular MBA course entitled *High-Stakes Leadership*. The course
has been a fixture at Michigan Ross for more than 30 years and offers
students the opportunity to explore — through real interactions,
not just case studies or textbooks — the experiences of seasoned
C-suite executives and the lessons each of those leaders has learned
from guiding their organizations through a major crisis. To date,
High-Stakes Leadership has welcomed, as our esteemed guests,
hundreds of chief executives from many of the world's most recog-
nizable brands. A fundamental lesson that has been shared by nearly
every visiting executive is the vital importance of understanding our
own personal values and then consistently behaving in ways that
demonstrate them. When students inevitably ask why values matter,
our guests generally respond with something like this:

> *Today's business environment is remarkably complex. While we
> aspire to deliver exceptional value to all our stakeholders, we
> don't always succeed. When we fall short, our ability to effectively
> lead is questioned. It can be hard for stakeholders to see and*

appreciate how our enterprise is trying to create value for them, especially when we're failing to meet their expectations. It is, however, easy for them to see the way we behave and the effort we put forth — or don't put forth — to engage with them.

To earn and maintain the trust and confidence of stakeholders, we must consistently and sincerely demonstrate our commitment to their interests. When our behaviors are aligned with our personal values, our actions are more consistent, they are executed with greater energy, and they are much more likely to be accepted as genuine.

Everyone knows when your actions are (or are not) true to what you really believe.

During each class, as students probe further into these claims, executives invariably describe two reasons why values-based actions are so important for today's leaders. First, they consistently point to the level of effort required to run a successful enterprise. Exceptional execution in any environment takes an incredible amount of dedication and energy. Clear alignment between the mission of an organization and the personal values of those leading it is imperative for maintaining the requisite level of effort over an extended period of time. It is this sustained effort, our guests contend, that ultimately enables an organization to remain highly competitive.

Second, the visiting executives point to the challenges of what I simply refer to as "the messiness of business" — often described by military leaders as the *volatile, uncertain, complex,* and *ambiguous* (*VUCA*) environments in which today's military units are typically required to operate. In these environments, resources are always constrained, information is never complete or perfect, and decision-making quality is paramount. In complex scenarios like these, leadership efforts must be focused on the implications of constantly changing conditions. This is *not* the time to be weighing the differences between *what needs to be done* and *what the organization wants me to do*. In high-performance organizations, the alignment of personal and organizational values takes place well in advance of having to face a crisis or even the everyday "messiness of business."

Bo Brabo and I share the experience of having learned a great deal about leadership, teamwork, and exceptional performance — particularly in VUCA environments — from our years of military service. From my own experience as the chief instructor at the U.S. Navy Fighter Weapons School (known to many as TOPGUN) and as a co-founder and executive at JetBlue Airways, I fully embrace the notion that leaders in any environment must have a clear sense of their values and how these very personal beliefs align (or don't) with the performance expectations of organizational leaders. When full alignment exists, leaders are free to be authentic and behave in ways that simply *feel right*. When some degree of misalignment exists, leaders often struggle with conflicting perspectives: "*Should I do what feels right to me? Or should I do what I think the organization wants me to do?*" When these two questions produce different answers, leaders will almost certainly find it difficult to consistently elevate the confidence of stakeholders.

Bo's book, *From the Battlefield to the White House to the Boardroom,* was written to help anyone with leadership responsibilities lead more effectively. Specifically, the book is a practical guide for developing your own values-based approach to leadership. As you will see in the pages that follow, Bo's unique combination of experiences on the battlefield, inside the beltway in Washington, DC, and as a seasoned business executive provide a rare breadth of perspective that make his recommendations universally applicable. If you are a military leader looking for a more effective way to connect your own leadership philosophy with the mission of your unit, this book will help you do so. Similarly, if you are a business leader in search of a mechanism for merging your personal values and the strategic plan of your enterprise, the pages that follow will show you the way.

Today's operating environments are, indeed, remarkably complex. To execute effectively, organizations must have leaders whose actions consistently earn the trust and confidence of their stakeholders. According to a rapidly growing body of research, the best way to ensure this consistency is through the thoughtful and explicit alignment of organizational values and the personal values of organizational leaders. Interested in learning how to move in this direction? Read on. You'll be glad that you did.

Cheers,
Mike Barger

PREFACE
An Ode to the Army Values

In nearly everything I do, I am guided by the seven values of the United States Army — Loyalty, Duty, Respect, Selfless Service, Honor, Integrity, and Personal Courage. These values have taken me from the battlefield to the White House to the boardroom. They have guided decisions I've made in the military, in government service, and in Corporate America. They influence the way I think and act and lead, at work and at home. And they inspired this book and the lessons that await you.

The United States Army guidon (i.e., its military standard or flag) currently carries 190 campaign (or battle) streamers that are draped from the top of the staff. Each streamer is less than three inches wide and is four feet long. These battle streamers are colorful, meaningful, and historic. They represent the "results" of millions of Soldiers over a quarter century, exemplifying the Army values of Loyalty, Duty, Respect, Selfless Service, Honor, Integrity, and Personal Courage. On the battlefield, at the most basic level, Soldiers fight for each other. The heroes who jump on grenades, those who keep fighting after being shot multiple times, those who know their life is in extreme jeopardy, and those who pay the ultimate sacrifice are demonstrating the absolute best of all the Army Values combined ... and then some!

The Army was founded on June 14, 1775. At the time of this book's publication, 245 years after its founding, the Army employs more than 1.3 million people (Active, Reserve, National Guard, and Civilians). Expand that to include the entire Department of Defense and that's a payroll of more than two million strong, giving Walmart a run for its money for the title of "largest employer in the United States."

So how does the Army — an organization with more than a million people — live by, exemplify, and maintain a strong values system?

How does generation after generation of Soldiers continue to carry out the nation's defense both at home and abroad? And what are the key takeaways others can use in their own organizations?

I have gleaned the answers to these questions through my career so far, and will endeavor to share my take with you throughout the pages of this book ... through stories and profiles and personal insights.

But it all comes down to one simple truth: Values drive results. Committing fully to admirable organizational values — up, down, and across an organization, every day and in every way, is a powerful formula for success.

It all comes down to one simple truth: Values drive results. Committing fully to admirable organizational values — up, down, and across an organization, every day and in every way, is a powerful formula for success.

CHAPTER 1
Values, Behavior, and Results

This book — *From the Battlefield to the White House to the Boardroom: Leading Organizations to Values-Based Results* — is the culmination of the 30+ years I have spent in these arenas as a leader, a follower, a student, an HR professional, a Soldier, and a Presidential Communications Officer for President George W. Bush and President Barack Obama. In the following pages, I've assembled tools and tips, numerous stories, interviews with organizational leaders, some facts and figures, and even some images and personal letters that might tug at your heartstrings. My hope is that this book helps you establish, build upon, or re-energize a values-based system for your organization or team. I hope you will come to see "more value" in the concept of workplace values. And I believe that leading your own team or company to a strong values-based system can and will lead to desired outcomes and an organizational culture worthy of emulation.

I believe that leading your own team or company to a strong values-based system can and will lead to desired outcomes and an organizational culture worthy of emulation.

Let's get down to business! First, this is not a book focused on CULTURE. Culture, in and of itself, is too often just a buzzword thrown around without substance, critical thought, or real understanding of how to *change* a culture, *build* a culture, or *maintain* a culture — keeping it just the way it is.

Culture matters, of course, but it's not what comes first. What I have learned is that culture is created by people … who exhibit behaviors (for better or for worse) over time, and those behaviors stem from or deviate from admirable (and sometimes stated) organizational values.

Let me share a formula that helps me think about the relationship between values, behavior, culture, and results.

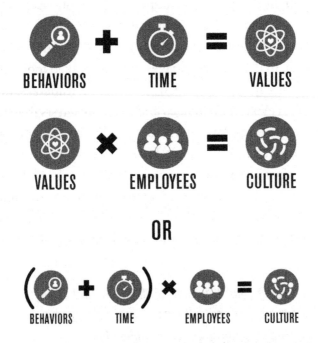

Organizational cultures, of course, are not as simple or impersonal as a mathematic equation, but the concept might help you appreciate the argument that to change cultures for the better, we need to change employee behaviors, and to change employee behaviors, we need meaningful and shared values to guide us. And, with luck, we'll have great leaders who step to the fore to keep us dedicated to those values, understanding why they matter — to our employees, our customers, our various stakeholders, our industry, and even to the world at large.

Think about your company, organization, department, or team. Now think about culture as something that arises, results, or emerges from the collective behaviors of all the employees in that company, organization, department, or team. Is the culture that results from all those behaviors — the decisions, the words, the actions — what you desire? Does it match the "core values" your organization has on its website, the office wall, or in the company strategic plan? If not, or if it's veering a bit off course, have faith. The equation works.

You see, if we were working out a math problem and get the answer wrong, we would go back to the work we did on the left side of the equation to find the error(s) and then work through them until we get the correct answer. Think about all the math classes you've taken in school, in which the teacher or professor tells you to be sure to "show your work." Why? They're looking for where you went right and where you went wrong when working out the problem on the left side of the equation. They're looking to give partial credit for what you did well and to offer guidance on how to fix what you did wrong.

Using this math analogy, if an organization doesn't have the culture it desires, it has to go back to the left side of the equation above — (Behaviors + Time) x Number of Employees = Culture — and figure out what behaviors aren't consistent with its values. It's a top-to-bottom review of employee behavior, meaning the behaviors of everyone must be examined (including and perhaps especially the behaviors of C-suite leaders). We must separate the desirable behaviors from those not desired and then take action to ensure sustainable improvement to those behaviors.

But what if people are, in fact, behaving in accordance with a shared set of values and the culture and overall business results are a mess? Then there may be an issue with the values themselves. Do the organization's leaders and/or key employees value a "win at any cost" approach to business? Do they value speed over quality? Do they value profit over people? Do they value popularity over truth?

The moment you sense that consistent behaviors are resulting in a less-than-admirable culture, it's time to review what went into establishing the organization's core values in the first place. It's also important to note the entire process of establishing core values is not a "set it and forget it" process. To achieve the desired culture (outcome), the process must be ingrained in the daily activities of the organization. This is why building and maintaining exemplary organizational cultures is much easier said than done. It takes genuine leadership at all levels, living and breathing the core values, and driving the effort within their teams to motivate and encourage others to do the same. In my career, I've seen this done well, and I've seen it fail. And I hope I've demonstrated values-based leadership to the people around me.

Establishing core values is not a "set it and forget it" process.

"Values-based leadership" and "values-based results" (a term I use in the subtitle of this book) is ultimately about what people *do* — not what they hope or pretend or intend or dream about. Behavior is where the rubber meets the road. Let me share an analogy as a final scene-setting exercise in this whole discussion about values-based behaviors and culture.

Imagine a traditional American Thanksgiving dinner — a day steeped in tradition, with cooks and bakers and hosts and guests ... all resulting in a sort of mini "culture." Imagine a family gathered around the table for turkey, stuffing, mashed potatoes, greens, casseroles, and more. Of course, there's pie for dessert and plenty of whipped cream. Now, what if the family all sat down around the table and the main dish, the turkey, was missing. Dad forgot to cook the turkey. *Whoa!* There's some serious breakdown somewhere and Dad is in trouble ... with the entire family. Somewhere along the way — leading up to Thanksgiving Day — Dad's behaviors fell short. We can't blame the turkey (part of the tradition/culture of the day). In that moment, all eyes are on Dad and his behaviors ... the left side of the equation. Behaviors by people create culture. Repeated behaviors — like if Dad forgets his cooking duties for every special holiday, month after month, year after year — tells us that Dad's values might not match up to our own, and that our "family holiday culture" is breaking down around us.

Apply the rationale to any group — a company, a neighborhood, a city, a state, a country, or even a family. It's the behaviors of the people therein that create the culture.

CHAPTER 2
The Battlefield
In the Beginning

On March 17, 1987, when I was 17 years old, I started my journey in the Michigan Army National Guard. Here's how it all began.

I was just a junior in high school and I remember the recruiter very clearly. I first saw him on career day at my school. He gave his speech and told the group of high school students that we should take the Armed Services Vocational Aptitude Battery (ASVAB) test. We could even take the test right there in the school library ... imagine that! Coming from a military family — my father having served in the Navy during Vietnam and my two grandfathers having served in the Army during World War II — I figured it was my turn.

I took the ASVAB test in the school library and then had a one-on-one meeting with the recruiter about a month later at his office. It was just me and him talking about the Army; I felt like I was immediately under his spell. Hanging on the walls (and on doors and just about everywhere) were posters of Soldiers shooting machine guns, driving tanks, jumping out of airplanes, maneuvering through obstacle courses. There were photos of more cool stuff than I could ever wrap my teenage brain around. Who wouldn't get super pumped to be part of all that? Then the recruiter asked the one question that would end up setting the course for my life: "What do you want to do in the Army?"

In that moment, I had no idea that my answer would dictate the trajectory of my life and career. I responded: "I want to get into business. Do you have anything that fits?"

Hold on a minute. What about all those cool posters? Where did that response come from? Honestly, I wasn't even sure. "Business" wasn't really on my radar, at least not consciously. I had roofed houses with my dad as a teenager and had held a part-time job as a dishwasher and busboy in a local restaurant, but nothing entrepreneurial as of yet. But I said it — "I want to get into business" — and the uniformed recruiter across the desk from me was well trained to "get the recruit." So he proceeded to open his regulation book (no internet back then, but plenty of books and manuals on his desk!) and go straight to the page that said, "Personnel Administration Specialist."

Wait, what? I had no clue what "personnel administration" was. With even more salesmanship, the recruiter proceeded to explain how "personnel administration" and "business administration" were essentially the same thing. I was 17, folks, and somehow it all made sense to me. But it would be many years before I realized they had pulled a business/human resources (HR) switcheroo on me, which paved my way into a lifetime of people management. Looking back, I'm so grateful for that moment of serendipity.

So, I had taken the aptitude test, chosen a "job," and my next step was to bring in my parents to give their consent, as I was still a minor. And the rest, as they say, is history!

The Mission

The Army Mission remains constant: "To deploy, fight, and win our nation's wars by providing ready, prompt and sustained land dominance by Army forces across the full spectrum of conflict as part of the joint force. The Army mission is vital to the nation because we are the service capable of defeating enemy ground forces and indefinitely seizing and controlling those things an adversary prizes most — its land, its resources, and its population."[1]

How is the Army mission achieved? How do Soldiers accomplish the mission when the bullets are flying? Easy. Hold true to your Army Values and execute how you were trained. Let's think outside of the Army for just a moment to add some context to why this is so important. Even think about your own company or companies you've worked for in the past. Are the company's values ingrained in absolutely everything the company does, as they are in the Army? Are there mandatory, company-wide training and development programs reflective of exactly how the company does business? When we believe in our organizational values and use them to drive our day-to-day behaviors and decision making, it's suddenly easier to achieve our mission (or seize upon financial success, profitable growth, employee retention, and more).

How do Soldiers accomplish the mission when the bullets are flying? Easy. Hold true to your Army Values and execute how you were trained.

Surely, there are many readers of this book who haven't served in the Armed Forces — whose "battles" have been waged in boardrooms or at nonprofits, in classrooms or court rooms or operating rooms, on

---

1   https://www.army.mil/about/

stages and anywhere else work is performed. This book is for you! The Army values are just one set of values to demonstrate how aligned behaviors — over time, by many employees — can create remarkable results. Take from here what you can use to better your workplace processes for training as you compete (i.e., fight) for a competent workforce, higher sales and revenue, higher profit margins, better quality products and services, and workplace behaviors that produce an amazing company culture.

Bootcamp

In June 1987, right after finishing my junior year of high school, I went to Fort Bliss, Texas, for basic combat training (i.e., boot-camp). This was during the heat of the summer. I was referred to as a "split-option trainee." I would attend bootcamp the summer after 11th grade, then back to high school, followed by individual skills training the summer after high school graduation. Today, I think of that experience as a unique exercise in "values training." Bootcamp brought together people from all across the country to mold them into Soldiers and to instill the same seven core values (Loyalty, Duty, Respect, Selfless Service, Honor, Integrity, and Personal Courage) in ALL of them. Why is that important? Follow along.

The most fascinating part of bootcamp is the gathering of new, fresh recruits into one organization — young men and women from anywhere and everywhere across the country, all looking to make a difference. In 1987, men and women were still going through bootcamp separately. My company of young men included different races, religions, backgrounds, cultures, socioeconomic privileges (or lack thereof), and even criminal histories. (Yes, the old cadence that included the lyric, "Join the Army or go to jail" was based in reality for many new recruits.) For the first time in my life, having lived in a predominantly white community, I was standing shoulder to shoulder with the real world. Not only was I raised in a community that lacked cultural diversity, I was raised in a home that never even *talked* about race, religion, politics, or anything outside of what was happening from day to day. So this was truly ALL new to me. *The Army! Wow! I have arrived!*

The most fascinating part of bootcamp is the gathering of new, fresh recruits into one organization — young men and women from anywhere and everywhere across the country, all looking to make a difference.

The moment us fresh recruits stepped off the bus in the training area at Fort Bliss, "they" were waiting for us. *Drill Sergeants!* And they were scary as hell. Tall ones, short ones, all with muscles galore and thundering vocal cords that made you feel as if God himself was yelling at you and that big trouble was about to rain down on your head. And it did. They didn't discriminate either ... no special treatment for any of us. Immediately, it seemed as if there were as many of them as there were of us, and there were about 200 of us. (In reality, there were only about 20 of them, but they were bigger than life and in full control.)

The Drill Sergeants were wearing their standard Drill Sergeant headgear (i.e., the brown round) and they used it to their advantage. If you're not familiar with the Drill Sergeant hat, it looks like a State Trooper hat or Smokey the Bear's hat; it's stiff and intimidating and can be used as a weapon. In those early days of bootcamp, I was hit so many times with the edge of the brown round I couldn't keep track. The Drill Sergeants would stand as close as they needed to ensure the edge of the brown round would hit you as they were screaming commands at you. In that moment, us recruits were all piss ants, shit bags, numb nuts, m'fers, c'suckers, no-good pieces of trash. In relatively short order, every single one of us was dressed down to a common person ... "Private!" (Sometimes I make myself laugh thinking about opening new employee orientation in Corporate America like this, but we all know where that would lead ... right to the unemployment line!)

During the eight weeks of intense bootcamp, the Drill Sergeants never let up and absolutely did what the Army needed them to do ... they turned us into Soldiers. We were Army green. They would never let you see them sweat and, in the end, you could see their pride in what they had accomplished. Their behaviors — every minute of every day — developed the desired behaviors in every single one of us. Those newly developed behaviors brought us to living and breathing the Army values. And, though I didn't understand or appreciate it then, operating from a shared set of behaviors would be the foundation for my entire life in leadership.

The Drill Sergeants never let up and absolutely did what the Army needed them to do ... they turned us into Soldiers.

Leadership 101

After bootcamp and advanced individual training (i.e., the Army's version of trade school), my first leadership program was the Primary Leadership and Development Course (PLDC). My four weeks in the PLDC were a profound time for me, as it was my introduction into formal leadership training. This course taught me the "Be, Know, Do" leadership framework of the Army. *Field Manual (FM) 22-100: Army Leadership*, would be a *New York Times* bestseller if it were published in such a fashion as leadership self-help books are today. And because we have Google, you can find it for free! (You're welcome. No bootcamp required.)

I was 26 at this point. This was after college, after my National Guard time had ended, and about two years after enlisting on active duty. It was PLDC that really helped me home in on the "Do" piece of leadership. After weeks of being yelled at and sometimes feeling paralyzed about what to do next, it was my time to take *action* ... time to *do*.

I went through PLDC at Camp Jackson, South Korea. South Korea has quite a bit of mountainous terrain and the terrain surrounding Camp Jackson did not disappoint. To develop each component of the Be, Know, Do, there was a process of building mental and physical toughness (Be), teaching technical and tactical skills (Know), and being tested on performing the skills (Do). One particular event had me in its crosshairs: land navigation. The instructors gave us a topographical map with terrain features, latitude and longitudinal lines, a compass, a protractor, a pencil, some paper, and grid coordinates. They taught us how to use it all in a classroom environment. I paid attention and it seemed simple enough ... until they opened the classroom door, pointed to the mountains, gave me four 8-digit grid coordinates and said "Go find them!"

If you're reading this and grew up only having known smartphones, Google Maps, GPS apps, and other way-finding tools, this "coordinates and a protractor" dilemma will be foreign to you. I had only my rudimentary tools and a set of very new skills regarding how to determine intersection and resection points on a map ... and I had three hours to find those four points. No phone, no radio, just a map ... now go! This was truly a high-anxiety, adrenaline-driven event. At one juncture, it even included leaving the base and traversing through a Korean concrete manufacturing facility in order to get to one of the grid coordinates. I often reflect on that and wonder what they must have thought of us. In the end, it took me almost the entire three hours to find the four points. It was an "up and down the mountainside, through the woods, to grandmother's house we go" kind of thing!

In the end, PLDC was an incredible confidence booster. It taught me that when faced with difficult tasks, I had to lean on the skills I had learned and go forth and conquer. Leadership means being out front, going first where you ask your teams to go. "Do as I do," not "do as I say."

Leadership means being out front, going first where you ask your teams to go. "Do as I do," not "do as I say."

It was only a few years later that I found myself in another, more daunting Army training course that would test me even further ... Airborne school.

Paratrooper Brabo

"Now that I have done my best, pin those wings upon my chest!" All these years later, I can still hear it — the line of a cadence sung on many a morning runs during Airborne school at Fort Benning, Georgia. There's so much I can share about Airborne school, but the Army perhaps frames it best:

> *The purpose of the Basic Airborne Course is to qualify the volunteer in the use of the parachute as a means of combat deployment and to develop leadership, self-confidence, and an aggressive spirit through mental and physical conditioning.*

> *Airborne Soldiers have a long and distinguished tradition of being an elite body of fighting men and women — people who have always set the example for determination and courage. When you volunteer for this training, you accept the challenge of continuing*

this tradition. The Airborne Soldiers of the past set high standards
— it is now up to you to maintain them![2]

I think the Army captured the description of the Paratrooper well. As many would say (with a hint of sarcasm), "Why would anyone want to jump out of a perfectly good airplane?" I, too, remember having this exact thought before having the opportunity to actually go do it. Without question, it was a time and an experience I will never forget.

"Why would anyone want to jump out of a perfectly good airplane?"

Unlike bootcamp and PLDC, I don't recall the names of my instructors in Airborne school. These Non-Commissioned Officers (NCOs) were different. They were "the Black Hats" — known for the black headgear (similar to a baseball cap) they wore, along with a black t-shirt with their unit logo on it and Army fatigue pants. Like Drill Sergeants, they were a bit intimidating with the physical stature of the Greek god Zeus. Given the thousands of airborne jumps the Black Hats had, they too could be thought of like the legend of Zeus and having control over the skies. Bottom line, these guys didn't need names ... they were Black Hats!

The Basic Airborne Course had just a few primary tasks: Learn how to exit the aircraft, execute emergency procedures if needed, and learn how to hit the ground without breaking a leg. I learned those things and did them all successfully, but what I learned about myself went well beyond.

---

2   https://www.goarmy.com/soldier-life/being-a-soldier/ongoing-
       training/specialized-schools/airborne-school.html

The Basic Airborne Course had just a few primary tasks: Learn how to exit the aircraft, execute emergency procedures if needed, and learn how to hit the ground without breaking a leg.

On the surface and with zero experience jumping out of airplanes, it seemed to me like a simple thing to accomplish. Training was just three weeks in duration ... who couldn't do that??? Well, that was an incredibly *long* three weeks and I was very quick to ask myself, *"Who am I?"* The course had 3 phases — ground week, tower week, and jump week. It seemed that the entire focus of the course was a proper parachute landing fall (PLF) and keeping your feet and knees together. But there was much more ... running everywhere we went, doing pull-ups each and every time we entered or left the barracks and, most of all, not dozens of PLFs, but hundreds ... maybe a thousand (all before ever jumping out of a plane)! We first learned to fall over from a standing position, then by stepping off a platform 3-feet-high, then stepping off a 10-foot platform wearing a parachute harness connected to a pully system all controlled by none other than a Black Hat who decided when to let you drop to the ground and .... you guessed it ... perform a proper PLF. Getting it wrong meant doing it right two times to make up for the wrong ... and on and on it went.

At the end of week one (ground week), when we finished our morning qualifying run and slowed down to a march, my right knee wouldn't bend. A Black Hat noticed and pulled me out of formation and sent me to the medical clinic. The doc said I had two options — get a medical profile (which would lead to dismissal from the course) or get of shot of cortisone in the right butt-cheek and drive on. This was the first *"Who am I?"* moment for me. Answer: *"I'm not a quitter and I'm not going back to the unit without jump wings, so give me the shot, doc!"*

By the end of week two (tower week), my left hip was so bruised from doing hundreds of PLFs that it looked like a slab of raw meat. Here comes *"Who am I?"* number two. Again, I was offered two basic options — go see the doc again and most likely get sent home, or suck it up. So I answered myself the same way and added prayer for healing and good winds during jump week ... I needed the kind of winds that would help me land on my *right* side!

Our last jump in the course was a jump with full combat gear at night ... in the dark ... can't see s**t ... the only thing to orient you being the sound of the rucksack hanging 50 feet below you from a rope when it finally hits the ground and you know you're next. Right thereafter we had our graduation ceremony. This was the perfect time. We were coming from the last jump with full adrenaline, and the Black Hats knew that was the time to "pin those wings upon our chest!" Having successfully made it through to graduation and having "earned" my wings was like nothing else I'd ever achieved. I am a U.S. Army Paratrooper. This was the accomplishment that spoke to me, *"Bo, you can **DO** anything you set your mind to."*

All throughout this course, Black Hats were leading us in every way. They trained us, motivated us, inspired us, kept us safe, and showed us what the Army value of Personal Courage was all about. Every jump was led by a Black Hat Jump Master. The Black Hat went first, led the way, did the "Do" as a way of teaching the rest of us to eventually "do" on our own. It's curious to me that I don't remember their names ... I sure do remember their character, courage, and ability to model the behaviors we needed to learn.

Candidate Brabo

As we get older, our stories and experiences stack up ... we have more years to look back upon. More years to analyze the decisions we made that led to traveling down one path or another, for better or for worse. And as the years go by, we're afforded more time to reflect upon the decisions and actions — of others and of ourselves — that may have put us on a certain path. This next story in my timeline is a pivotal one and truly set the stage for where I am today.

In 2003, while serving my first tour with the White House Communications Agency, I was blessed with being selected to join the Army Warrant Officer ranks. During that selection year for my specialty, Human Resources (i.e., the glorious HR word and no longer "personnel administration"), the Army had 12 slots to fill and more than 60 applicants. To be one of the 12 was a true honor. After selection, I was off to Warrant Officer Candidate School (WOCS).

During my tenure in the Army, WOCS was considered like a bootcamp on steroids. *"How bad could it really be?"* I asked, *"There aren't any Drill Sergeants!"* But there were Training, Advising, and Counseling (TAC) Officers ... all of whom were Warrant Officers themselves. Ever heard of "an Officer and a Gentleman?" TAC Officers must be gentlemen too, right? I assure you that, outside of the schoolhouse, they most surely are. Inside the schoolhouse from the candidate's perspective, the TAC Officer is there to make you miserable, push you to your most outer limits (physically and mentally), and drive you in to the ground until you truly understand how to perform together as a highly cohesive team.

The TAC Officer is there to make you miserable, push you to your most outer limits (physically and mentally), and drive you in to the ground until you truly understand how to perform together as a highly cohesive team.

Have you ever heard TEAM defined as "Together Everyone Achieves More?" In Corporate America, on college campuses, on athletic fields, and just about everywhere else, thinking of a team in the context of "together everyone achieves more" is pretty prevalent. And it just makes good sense. In WOCS, this concept of teamwork is paramount. We had individual tasks and collective tasks, and the collective tasks were designed to be unachievable unless candidates were working together to get them done. We were challenged to split up collective tasks so we could each contribute to our collective success. Everything we were asked to do was impossible to accomplish without the assistance of others, but if we were caught physically helping someone with their *individual* tasks, we were apt to see the exit door due to an honor code violation. It's not a game of cat and mouse. TAC Officers don't play games. It's about critical thinking in an arduous environment, setting priorities, managing risk, and putting the team ahead of yourself. WOCS mastered the art of teaching and influencing others to perform selflessly, exemplifying the Army value of Selfless Service.

Let me set the scene. There were 60 people, men and women, living on the third floor of a three-story barracks building — two to four people per room; men with men, women with women. All rooms were on a single long hallway with a separate male and female latrine centered in the middle of the hall. There was an exit at the end of the hallway to an exterior staircase.

Come with me back to this experience. Here's your first task starting on day one. You must sleep *under* the sheets and blankets in your bed. If you try to get a jump-start on the day by sleeping on *top* of the blanket so you don't have to make your bed in the morning, you'll get expelled for an honor code violation (trying to get one over on your fellow candidates). Wake up is at 0535 (5:35 a.m.) and the first formation of the day for physical fitness training is at 0542 (5:42 a.m.). That's a whopping seven minutes to do all of the following — with the requirement that the entire group, all 60 candidates, must exit the hallway using the exterior staircase TOGETHER as a group:

- Wake up
- Get out of bed
- Put PT gear on
- Unlock wall locker, grab toothbrush and toothpaste
- Lock wall locker (must always be locked when not in the room)
- Walk down hallway to latrine (no running allowed)
- Use latrine and brush teeth
- Walk down hallway back to room
- Unlock wall locker and store toothbrush and toothpaste
- Make bed
- Prep wall locker drawers for inspection
- Line up in hallway at exit door
- Ready for exit
- Be standing in formation as a group, right at 0542 (not early, not late).

When's the last time you got out of bed without snoozing the alarm and did anything in seven minutes, other than stumble to the bathroom? Our group wasn't able to accomplish all that either, and there was punishment for being late to formation. The Commander of the 1st Warrant Officer Company would start the day right at 0542. When we showed up late, he would pause, thank us for finally showing up (sarcastically, of course), and put us immediately into the front leaning rest position (i.e., a push-up or plank position with arms fully extended). He would purposely take at least another five minutes before releasing the various groups of candidates to do their fitness training. Ever held a plank, even on your elbows, for more than five minutes? It sucks, both physically and mentally!

After a few days of being late and finally coming together in group consensus and simply saying "enough is enough," we started to use our brains and think through the performance of all the tasks I outlined above. We came up with an efficiency process that we would all follow in order to get everything done in our allotted seven minutes and be right on time to formation. On day five, we made it and never missed 0542 formation for the rest of the course.

How did we do it? Personal hygiene. The morning of day four, we crafted a memo requesting authorization to carry our toothbrushes and toothpaste in our bookbags so we could brush our teeth in the schoolhouse after lunch. It was approved. We used the importance of personal hygiene as a tool to eliminate tasks on the list. On day five, we woke up and instead of having to go through the unlocking and locking of the wall locker to get the toothbrush and toothpaste, we rolled out of bed and put our hands in our bookbags and went straight to the latrine. This one change easily shaved 90 seconds off the task list.

This is just one example and a fun illustration to share. What was the point of this exercise? The very first task of the day was impossible to accomplish without teamwork and loyalty to each other. If one person can finish the tasks in four minutes but the others can't, who cares? He can't go to formation without the other 59 candidates. It illustrates the "I have your back ... I'll watch your six ... I'll move out and draw fire, cover me" kind of trust and steadfast loyalty needed on the battlefield. The Army value of Loyalty is a deep one. It's responsible for the lifelong bonds and camaraderie active duty Soldiers and Veterans alike experience.

The very first task of the day was impossible to accomplish without teamwork and loyalty to each other.

Combat – Iraq 2004

After I finished Warrant Officer Candidate School and the Warrant Officer Basic Course thereafter, I was destined for Kitzingen, Germany, with my family in tow. A big move for us all. My daughters Clara and Ellen were 5 and 10 years old at the time. The cat (Princess) came along too; Princess added some normalcy to our new "home front." Not only was it a move, it was a move to a foreign country where we lived in a small village and didn't speak the language. One of the greatest strengths of a seasoned Soldier is adaptability — and Army brats, as our children are often called, learn adaptability too. My girls made friends, went to school on base, and played in the village with the local kids. Their level of resiliency impressed me.

My assignment was to Alpha Detachment (Alpha Knights), 38th Personnel Services Battalion, supporting the 1st Infantry Division. The Division was tapped to deploy to combat operations in Iraq for Operation Iraqi Freedom II (2nd wave following the 4th Infantry Division out of Fort Carson, Colorado). Our detachment was led by Captain Luis A. Parilli (aka Pretty Tony — trust me, that's a term of endearment from our First Sergeant, Robert E. "Top" Ducksworth). CPT Parilli (Colonel today) was a handsome young West Pointer who was, without a doubt when looking back over my career in the Army, the best leader I ever had the honor of serving with. And I certainly can't leave out our Lieutenant, Marci Strathearn, who carried unbelievable pressure in railhead operations, troop movement and logistics, and leading Soldiers in combat. The four of us — me, Tony, Robert, and Marci — were a team of all teams. We would have made the late Michigan Wolverines football coach, Bo Schembechler, proud as we lived his motto … The Team, The Team, The Team! (As a recent Michigan grad school alum, I say that with pride.)

Our deployment started at zero-dark thirty, when myself and my advance team stepped on a bus taking us to Nuremberg airport to process through debarkation operations and get on a plane to Kuwait. When I got on that bus, my family was there to see me off. The heartache was intense. This wasn't saying goodbye for a business trip or going to a school. This was goodbye with a prayer to Jesus that he brings me home one day so I could see them again.

When I got on that bus, my family was there to see me off. The heartache was intense. This wasn't saying goodbye for a business trip or going to a school. This was goodbye with a prayer to Jesus that he brings me home one day.

No matter what you do or have done for a living, we all go through life knowing that any day could be our last. But rarely do we head out the door for work in the mornings thinking there's an enemy waiting to kill us however he can. Rarely do we wonder if we'll be home for dinner (though I suspect police officers and their families might fear this every day). For me, leaving for Iraq was unlike any other "morning commute" I'd taken. Going to a war zone *knowing* there was an enemy waiting to kill me put a whole new meaning to saying goodbye to a loved one.

The flight to Kuwait was uneventful and we got to work immediately. After the advance team and I set up HR operations on Camp Wolverine in Kuwait City, we jumped on a Black Hawk and flew north to Balad, Iraq, and then on to Tikrit. When we arrived at the airfield on the outskirts of the city, controlled by the U.S. Army, it was in the pitch darkness of night. Of course, there were no lights and the chopper "landing" wasn't much more than a touch-n-go — maybe 20 seconds for my team to pitch bags out the side and get out, then back in the air it went.

No more did we hit the ground and we heard machine gun fire nearby. We hit the deck, huddled, and did our best to stay calm. Folks, we had no ammo, no idea where we were, no idea where the rest of our unit was (let alone how we were going to get there), and, oh by the way, it's pitch black and the only thing lighting up the sky was the occasional tracer round from the machine gun fire. If we weren't trained Soldiers, it would have been as good a time as any to panic!

We were a team and we had a mission. Our eyes started to adjust to the darkness and we were able to make out the silhouette of the airfield operations building. We stayed low to the ground and moved out. We found the ops team in the building and were able to make contact with our unit. Welcome to Iraq!

Keep It Light

In times of despair, laughter can be good medicine for the soul. I want to take a moment to recognize two of my Soldiers who had such God-given talent to make people laugh: Sydney Williams and Joey Ellington. Picture this ... a decrepit, rusted-out, metal container sitting on four wheels (technically a trailer) with a giant water bag sitting on the ground outside. There was a pump running off a generator, which pushed the water to the container. The container had a few stairs on the outside that led up to a door. Inside the container there were the most awful shower stalls you can imagine — about 8 of them. But on a positive note, IT WAS A SHOWER in the Iraqi desert!

Well, inside that container is where the comedy erupted. I termed it the "Shower Hour with Joey E & Lil'Sip." The banter back and forth would have me laughing so hard my sides hurt. If we had had smart phones with a YouTube channel back then, it would have been a hit. It was in those moments that Sergeant Williams and Specialist Ellington made us forget we were in a war zone! Those friends created some of my best memories in the battlefield, using their talents to keep morale high and making the stressors of war a little less each and every day.

Flying High, Flying Low

My movement from Kuwait to Iraq, around Iraq, and from Iraq back to Germany was all in the air. Black Hawks, Chinooks, and a C120. I never once was in a convoy. Looking back and given the number of killed and wounded Service members due to improvised explosive devices (IEDs) exploding under their vehicles, I consider myself extremely lucky.

During my many flights between Forward Operating Base (FOB) Speicher, on the outskirts of Tikrit, and FOB Danger, a former Saddam Hussein compound in the city that sat along the Tigris River, I often sat next to the door gunner and had a bird's-eye view of the terrain below. I also learned during these flights that there was a distinct difference between a regular active duty pilot and a National Guard pilot. For whatever reason, the National Guard pilots, older Warrant Officers like me, treated the chopper ride like a roller coaster ride at Six Flags! Up, down, left, right, dive, climb, land. Imagine flying fast about 100 feet above the ground, then there's a cliff — with the river about 70 feet below — and with a swift move, the pilot drops the chopper to just a few feet off the water. Without warning, another swift move and the chopper climbs 80 feet, banks hard right and does a slam-dunk landing on the helipad at the top of another cliff. Thank you, passengers, for riding the Army's friendly skies today ... we hope you enjoy the rest of your day (friendly sarcastic potshot at my fellow Warrant Officer brethren).

I think they had two intentions ... evade being an easy target for the enemy and making those tagging along for a ride want to puke!

On those chopper rides, flying low, I saw parts of Iraq that I hope one day will be filled with peace and shared with the world. Kids playing outside of their homes, which were little more than huts, skies in the distance that were brown because the air was filled with dust from desert windstorms (there was a beauty in that), and a vibrant Tigris River with green landscapes that would make for amazing resort property. It was on those rides that I often felt the true meaning of the value of Selfless Service. Away from the comforts of home, we were "putting others before self," beyond the team of Soldiers around us, and hoping to positively impact the people and the children in the world below.

On those chopper rides, flying low, I saw parts of Iraq that I hope one day will be filled with peace and shared with the world.

Honor the Fallen

I think I could write an entire book or make a movie based on my experiences and stories from the battlefield. But that's not the intent of this book, wherein I hope readers see the value in the "values" on display from the few stories written here. It's my opinion that the most important Army value is that of Honor. Here's how the Army defines it:

> *"Live up to Army values. The nation's highest military award is The Medal of Honor. This award goes to Soldiers who make honor a matter of daily living — Soldiers who develop the habit of being honorable, and solidify that habit with every value choice they make. Honor is a matter of carrying out, acting, and living*

the values of respect, duty, loyalty, selfless service, integrity and
personal courage in everything you do."[3]

There's a group of men and women who paid the ultimate sacrifice
and put their Honor on display for the world to see. And it's my honor
to recognize all who gave their lives during this, our modern-day
war, in Operation Enduring Freedom, Operation Iraqi Freedom,
and Operation New Dawn. You can find their names at TheFallen.
MilitaryTimes.com. Rest in peace, brother and sister in arms. You are
not forgotten!

---

3   https://www.army.mil/values/

CHAPTER 3
The Battlefield
The Relationships That Change Us

Iraq 2004 was a special time in my life. And what made it so special were the people and the place. All around me, I witnessed people living and breathing the Army values every day. We watched each other's back, took care of each other, and picked each other up when we were down. At the time of the publishing of this book, it's 16 years later and these are the people whose calls I answer, day or night, any day of the year. Special? No. They're beyond special.

Captain Tony Parilli and First Sergeant Robert Ducksworth — Standing Tall!

First Sergeant Ducksworth — Tired ... Needs a Nap!

Captain Tony Parilli and First Sergeant Robert Ducksworth led the way. All the Soldiers under the leadership of these two gentlemen survived combat in Iraq because they trained us, prepared us, stood side-by-side with us, and led from the front, always.

Warrant Officer Brabo (me) and Private Jamie Holder — Bald was easy; twins, maybe?

Private Jamie Holder was my mini-me. I was 34 in this photo and Jamie was around 18 or 19. Regardless of age, we shared in the "one team, one fight" mission.

Working out in the gym trailer at FOB Speicher was a regular activity for Soldiers at our base. Staying fit and healthy was important for many reasons, but the gym also symbolized the time to escape the realities of the day. We could take out the mental anguish on the weights and get it all out.

Cleaning weapons is a Soldier's task first performed in bootcamp after each range day and then it follows the Soldier through his or her entire Army career. Cleaning weapons in Iraq was a daily war-fighter duty. Dust from the desert sands had its way of getting into every nook and cranny imaginable in our weapons,

First Sergeant Ducksworth and Captain Parilli — Lightweights ☺

Private First-Class Dean Precourt — Train hard and the face just does that!

and the work was never done. So why not make it a team effort? Together, this important chore got done and, of course, there was back and forth banter to keep morale on high!

Another thing Soldiers are subject to is the ever-popular Army immunization program (I lost count of

Weapons cleaning was a team-building event.

the number of injections I received over 26+ years). To protect against a malaria outbreak while in Iraq, we all took a daily dose of medication. Hey, another opportunity to build camaraderie! On a serious note, this was done as a group to show equality and that no one was exempt. Integrity on display.

Even in the combat zone, human resource operations were in full swing seven days a week. Staying up to date on compliance, performance management, promotions, and casualty operations was paramount

Taking anti-malaria meds was yet another team-building event.

in accomplishing our mission. We had a duty to support the 1st Infantry Division task force and that's exactly what we did.

There's nothing like getting a letter or a package from home. Have you ever thought about how the letter or package gets to a Soldier in the middle of a war zone? Well, it's planes, pallets, forklifts, sorting warehouses, metal containers on flatbed trucks driven by Soldiers around Iraq ... all to get the mail from loved ones to their Soldiers far from home and in harm's way.

HR Training on FOB Speicher — Mission first, people always

HR operations overseas, including war zones, includes taking on the role of the U.S. Postal Service. One of the units within our personnel battalion was a postal company. We had a large sorting warehouse on FOB Speicher. So much mail was coming in that our HR team would augment the postal company after dinner chow to help unload pallet after pallet of packages and get them in the appropriate metal shipping containers for the truckers to

First Lieutenant Marci Strathearn, Postal and Logistics Leader Extraordinaire

take them out the next morning to other FOBs in the region. An act of Selfless Service to support the morale of others. It's who we were; it's who we are.

Mail every day. Lots of mail.

Think about how our behavior to support the postal company compares with the following corporate office example (an experience I personally had). The UPS delivery driver brings a few packages to the corporate office and they're received by an employee that answers the door, who then proceeds to set the packages on the floor near the entrance. It's a 5,000-square-foot office with 30 employees. First, it wouldn't have taken that employee more than a few minutes to place

the packages on the desks of the people they were addressed to, but that's not what happened here. Second, I let a couple days go by to see if

Oh, the mail! Sorting it all out.

anyone would pick up the packages and deliver them, but no one did. There didn't seem to be a care in the world about where those packages belong. On day three, I picked up the packages and delivered them. Small acts completed for others are sometimes insignificant in the eyes of the passerby.

Brown, sandstorm-filled sky over Tikrit.

TIP

If you see something that needs to be done and you have the ability and time to do it, be selfless and do it. It's just that simple.

Thousands of my fellow brothers and sisters in arms fought and died in this place called Iraq. Having stood on this land and sharing it with

Former Saddam Hussein palace in Tikrit.

you here gives me — and I hope you — a deeper level of gratitude for their sacrifice. It's that level of commitment to their country and

Another Saddam Hussein palace in Tikrit ... there were many!

their willingness to give their lives that I want you ... in Corporate America, in nonprofit management, in higher education, or wherever you work ... to grab onto and drive in your organizations. Give it all you have for the betterment of others and live by a set of core values that leads to results never seen before. When revenues, profit margins, and stock prices are viewed as they should be — as results that happen when we focus on driving the right behaviors — watch out world, that's a company about to soar!

Letters from Home

In those pallets full of mail there were sometimes letters from children and adults we'd never met — Americans of all ages sending us cheer and love and thanks. Those letters meant the world to me. So, with thanks to everyone who took the time to wish us well — including 2nd and 3rd graders in Texas, like Johnny, Juan, Kandis, Mericanmen, Michael, and Stephanie — I share with you here just a few of the letters (and drawings!) that helped boost our morale when we were far from home, doing difficult and meaningful work, and testing our commitment to the seven Army values that bonded us to one another.

Hi from Texas,

I am in seconed grade my name is Kandis I have been thinking about you alot. I live in Texas I am happ to give you candy for keeping us sate.

From Kandis

April 29, 04

Dear Robert Brabo,

How are you doing? I hope you are alright.
I pray for all of the soldiers that are fighting
for our country. I pray for their families too.
I hope you can come back to your family soon.
I know you miss them and they miss you
By the way, I am in third grade
at Edwin J. Kiest school. All of my class-
mates passed the Reading test

Sincerly
Maricanmen

Dear Robert,

How are you doing? I hope you're not lonely. My name is
Juan. I like like to play basketball with my friends. I'm
in third grade. I go to Edwin J. Kiest elematary school in Dallas
Tx. I like to read and to do math. What sport do you like?
What do you like to do? Are you happy being a soldier? I also
like animals. My favorite animals are horses, puppies, and Jaguars.
What is your favorite animal or animals?

From,

Juan

2611 Healey Dr
Dallas Tx 75228
May 5 2004

Dear Robert Brabo,
     Hi my name is Micheal Rodr-
iguez. I am nine and I'll month and 5
days. How is it over in Iraq y smacky?
How are you doing over there? I feel
very very sorry for the people who
die. Did you want to go or
was it a flash back. But
here's a little joke to tell the
Iraq y's. Joke time: Knock knock
who's there Boo Boo who? you better
cry when I win with my super dedween
team. Is it a good joke. If you
dont like it im fine with it I
gave you a drawing of me with
a back ground full of colorful fimorks.
I bet you a cool soldeir I bet.
Well I bet I'll have to say
Bye-Bye. Well write to you later
Bye-Bye.

                    You Friend
                Micheal Rodrguez

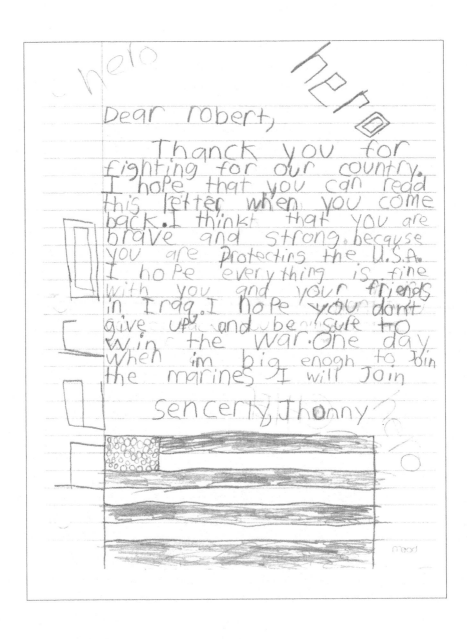

5-6-04

Dear Mr. Bravo,

My Name is Stephanie Giron Iao to Edwin J kiest Elementary. I am in 2nd grade.

My Parents are from El Salvador I was born in December 8, 1995. and I live in Dallas

I am glad that you are fighting for our freedom I bet your family is missing you a lot.

Sincerely

Stephanie

CHAPTER 4

Values in Action

Insights from Mike Barger, JetBlue Airways Co-Founder and Former Navy TOPGUN Pilot and Instructor

In my career and in my life, I've met countless admirable leaders. In addition to all those fellow Soldiers, White House staffers, and corporate colleagues I'm introducing you to through my stories are a few others who have inspired me in meaningful ways. Mike Barger, Rachel Noble, and Dan Denison are notable leaders I've bumped into in my journey of talking about, studying, and celebrating behaviors in the workplace, core values, and culture.

When I think about Mike, Rachel, and Dan, I think of them as very important leaders who exemplify what I call "values-based leadership." I had the honor to spend hours with, and even work with, Mike, Rachel, and Dan and am profiling them here in my book because they are three of the most talented, gifted, and humble people I've ever met. Given their accomplishments in life, they should have egos the size of Mount Rushmore. But they don't. These are people who help others be better, know better, and do better. They're inspirational. They're open with their life stories, all of which were shared with me (and now, with you) with the utmost kindness and sincerity.

Given their accomplishments in life, they should have egos the size of Mount Rushmore. But they don't.

In the following pages, in profiles woven between the narratives of my own leadership journey, let me introduce you to Mike Barger, Rachel Noble, and Dan Denison. Mike's leadership at JetBlue, Rachel's counsel to thousands of patients and corporate execs, and Dan's guidance to billion-dollar behemoths around the world all support the rationale that values drive results. When companies are aligned from top to bottom and bottom to top on their core values and the demonstrated behavior therein, the results can be nothing less than significant.

Values drive results. When companies are aligned from top to bottom and bottom to top on their core values and the demonstrated behavior therein, the results can be nothing less than significant.

Mike Barger

I first met Mike when I was a full-time Executive MBA student at the University of Michigan (*Go Blue!*) Ross School of Business, while still working full-time as an HR executive (August 2017 to May 2019). My cohort was privileged to have Mike deliver a fireside chat to our class about crisis management that really focused on his leadership in the wake of the terrorist attacks on September 11, 2001. Today, Mike is a professor at Ross, teaching 2nd-year MBA students all about that very subject: crisis management. Back then, though, he was with JetBlue Airways, but he wasn't just a crewmember or crew-leader (the terms they use for their employees and executives). He was a co-founder of the airline. On 9/11 and the days and months thereafter, airline travel — and the industry as a whole — changed forever. Leadership through these tragic times was front and center. Employees were uncertain, passengers were fearful, security was on heightened alert, and the news outlets were running airline-related stories 24/7. How did Mike and JetBlue get through it all? Read on …

On 9/11 and the days and months thereafter, airline travel — and the industry as a whole — changed forever. Leadership through these tragic times was front and center.

Prior to Mike co-founding JetBlue, he had risen to the top of his game as a United States Navy pilot. I like to think I know the real "Maverick and Viper" from the movie *Top Gun*! Prior to Mike separating from the Navy, he was a TOPGUN pilot and instructor. Tom Cruise and Tom Skerritt, the actors who played Maverick and Viper, have nothing on Mike Barger! Fighter pilots are the elite, rulers of the sky. How elite, you might ask? The 2018 Department of Defense Manpower Requirements Report for Fiscal Year 2018 (published online[1]) showed a total military end strength (military speak for "number of employees") of 1,314,000 active duty members, with the total authorized positions for fighter pilots during the same year being just 5,825. That's barely one half of one percent (0.0044). And there are shortages anywhere from 12 to 25% across the Air Force, Navy, and Marine Corps alike. Folks, that's way more elite than any pro athlete … ever. From one Veteran to another, THANK YOU for your service Mike.

It was during that initial fireside chat with Mike and our MBA class that I knew I wanted to hear and learn more about Mike's experience. Now fast forward a few months after graduation and I'm in the moment of reaching out to Mike to ask if he'd be willing to talk to me

---

[1]   https://prhome.defense.gov/Portals/52/Documents/MRA_Docs/TFM/Reports/ Final%20FY18%20DMRR%2011Dec2017.pdf?ver=2018-02-03-141625-140

about my book project (this book) and possibly write the foreword. Before actually sending the email, I sat at my desk for about an hour pondering what to say, how to say it, and playing a mental game against myself (me taking on myself and wondering what I would do). The whole point of this book is to highlight behaviors in the workplace and learn how to break through challenges and excel from the experiences, stories, and mentorship of others (me included). To learn "how" to do the DO, if you will.

While sitting there, contemplating the email to Mike and getting the nerve to actually hit the "send" button, it really boiled down to four possible outcomes:

1. I don't send it, so it's an automatic no.

2. He doesn't respond, so it's a no.

3. He responds and says no.

4. He responds and says YES.

Worst case, he says no ... wherein I haven't lost anything as I hadn't given anything to lose. And best case, he says yes. I was winning the battle with myself; there was a 25% chance of getting a yes and if I got it, the benefits would be immeasurable ... friendship, camaraderie, mentorship, guidance, and more. Hit the send button, Bo! And I won the battle with myself.

Mike and I met several times early in the morning before the demands of the workday were upon us. What follows is a synopsis of those pre-dawn chats, what I gleaned from them, and the message every reader can take and put in their toolkit.

When Mike separated from the Navy, it felt like a natural transition for him. After multiple deployments and with a growing family, he felt the time was right. I'm sure all our fellow military comrades and their families can relate to those sentiments firsthand. At the time, Mike's brother Dave was running Continental Airlines. The two talked about starting a new company and in a nutshell, it went a little something like this ...

> *"If we can assemble the right people, have a willingness to work as a team, figure out new ways to run an airline, be willing to take risks, then start a company that would treat customers and fellow crewmembers differently than they've experienced in the past, it's what we'd set out to do."*

There you have it, the idea that led to the founding of JetBlue Airways.

All startups start with an idea. Getting the idea through the barriers of entry to the market, to a product or service that can be sold, is where the rubber meets the road. Anyone can have a great idea, but the magic happens when business planning, strategy, and marketing meet execution through day-to-day business operations. How did JetBlue do it? How'd they build up their crewmembers? Let's see.

All startups start with an idea.

Building a Business Poses Problems to Solve

JetBlue's co-founder and initial Chief Executive Officer, David Neeleman, along with brothers Mike Barger and Dave Barger, challenged their first human resources executive, Ann Rhoades, to go find the right people. There was a problem to solve. It was tied to the very first thing Mike and Dave said in their initial idea statement ... *"if we can assemble the right people."* Ann put a two-day strategy meeting on the calendar to figure it out. This was about six months into the official start of the company and their crewleader count (JetBlue calls their executives "crewleaders" and their employees "crewmembers") was roughly 30, all of whom were to take part in the strategy session.

Mike described the first half of the first day as a little chaotic and they were getting nowhere fast. I can imagine, as I'm sure you can too, a strategy session not going in the right direction. Halfway through that first day, Ann broke the ice with a simple, yet formidable comment: *"Let's take a moment and figure out what's NOT working in the airline industry."* Ann's comment resonated deeply with every crewleader in the room. They had either come from other airlines or were customers/travelers of various airlines and were ripe to offer their opinions.

After Ann suggested that the team talk about all the things that weren't working in the airline industry, they began to list the things that they didn't like — issues that they collectively thought needed to be resolved or improved. A member of the team began to document these thoughts on sheets of butcher block paper on the walls of the large conference room. For the next five hours, the JetBlue leadership team added items to their list until the entire conference room was covered in paper and ideas. A copy of these items was provided to each crewleader, and their homework that first night was to think about *solutions* to as many of those issues as possible.

They returned the next day, ready to turn ideas into insights. JetBlue leaders began sharing their solutions to the challenges they had identified the previous day. Surprisingly, throughout the morning, they were able to agree on a solution to almost every one of them. As their discussion moved so quickly and they were finding it remarkably easy to resolve some of the airline industry's most common points of frustration for customers and employees, Dave Barger said "So, it feels like what we're doing here is just the radical application of common sense," which, naturally, became a cornerstone of JetBlue's culture from that point forward.

Once they had the walls of the conference room filled with both industry "opportunities" and JetBlue solutions, the team decided that they should try to group them, to make it easier to share the story of how JetBlue was planning to be different from every other airline. They were crafting a story that could be told to investors, to customers, and to new crewmembers. They were articulating a story that would ultimately be translated into their competitive strategy.

The JetBlue team ended up with five groups of challenges and solutions. "If we had to put labels on each of these groups," asked Ann, "how would we label them?" In fairly short order, the team had arrived at Safety, Caring, Integrity, Fun, and Passion.

These "labels," Mike explained to me during our interview, became JetBlue's Core Values — "not only to describe what we believed as a leadership team, but also how we were going to successfully compete. It was truly a breakthrough moment for the company."

These weren't just five words that were posted on the walls around JetBlue — these five core values drove their leadership philosophies, their corporate strategy, and their day-to-day operations. *Safety, Caring, Integrity, Fun, Passion.* And that's precisely what I believe great leaders do — they are driven by their values in every way, every day.

Great leaders are driven by their values in every way, every day.

Values in Action

In the months that followed, JetBlue incorporated these non-negotiable core values into everything from investor presentations and hiring processes to training programs and performance management practices. That was 1999 and, as of the publication of this book in 2020, those same core values are in place today.[2] The way JetBlue's values are explained on the airline website could have been taken directly from my chats with Mike. Mike said:

> *"JetBlue's values paint a clear picture for all new crewmembers. They're infused in their recruiting, hiring, training, operations, and performance management. It's these values that led JetBlue to its goal of 'bringing humanity back to air travel,' a quote attributed to David Neeleman."*

An integral part of the JetBlue story — and why I believe the five core values developed very early on are still intact — is leadership. About two years into the company's existence, Mike was leading the leadership and development group. It was then that JetBlue initiated annual crewmember feedback surveys, which they called the "Annual Speak-up Survey." With the first survey, he and his team identified a theme in the feedback:

> *"My supervisor isn't supporting me."*

The team saw a real leadership gap, mostly attributed to quick internal promotions due to the fast pace at which JetBlue was growing. They realized they needed to develop a set of guiding leadership principles that would align with their core values. Here's one quick story Mike shared that I absolutely loved because it's so real and applicable to just about *every* workplace. The names I use in the story are fake.

Suzy is a crewmember constantly late for work. Her supervisor, Jake, tells her repeatedly that her shift starts at 8:00 a.m. and she can't be late. Suzy, who is a good crewmember at work, tells Jake that she is

---

2   http://work-here.jetblue.com/category/get-to-know-us/

a single mom and has to take her child to daycare before starting work but the daycare doesn't open until 8:00 a.m., the same time she's supposed to start her shift. Therefore, Suzy consistently arrives at work late, but no later than 8:30 a.m. Jake never had a response other than "you're late" and had no idea how to handle the issue.

As Mike told me this story, it resonated with me that this is a story that I would bet applies to about every workplace out there. JetBlue found that Jake and other supervisors like him didn't know how to handle situations like this and JetBlue hadn't equipped them to do so. The quick promotions due to the company's fast growth led to crewmembers being co-workers one day and supervisor/subordinate the next. This story illustrates a common yet simple leadership problem that's foundational at its core. Foundational problems left unresolved are the ones that grow into monumental problems down the road. To fix this problem and mitigate others from developing, Mike and his leadership and development (L&D) team went to work.

Foundational problems left unresolved are the ones that grow into monumental problems down the road.

Mike and his team put together a proposal to pitch to JetBlue executive leadership. In partnership with the entire JetBlue leadership team, JetBlue University (the corporate learning function at the company) developed five leadership principles aligned with the five core values that were needed to help guide supervisors across the company on the *behaviors* (there's that word again) they should embody in order to demonstrate those values. The 5 leadership principles they came up with are:

1. Communicate with your team

2. Do the right thing

3. Treat your people right

4. Encourage initiative and innovation

5. Inspire greatness in others.

The L&D team defined these five leadership principles as "aspirational." They challenged the JetBlue executive leadership team to do three things with the principles:

- Know them
- Do them
- Teach them.

If that's not a call to action, I don't know what is. I wrote a sentence earlier about doing the DO. In Chapter 10, I'll dive into the "how," but I'll point out now that Mike and his team kept it simple ... and simple is key. Unlike other companies that tend to complicate matters, there was no 21-point action plan here ... it's three responsibilities ... KNOW, DO, TEACH. If you've been in organizations that make it too complex, it's often because leaders get in their own way; they're too smart for simple and it prevents real progress from happening.

If you've been in organizations that make it too complex, it's often because leaders get in their own way; they're too smart for simple and it prevents real progress from happening.

Each of the five leadership principles at JetBlue came with a story, examples, and history from JetBlue, and specific behavior elements associated with them. Implementing them did three very critical things:

1. Provided a set of guidelines for supervisors to use.

2. Gave JetBlue an opportunity to provide every crewmember the leadership blueprint on what to expect from their supervisors.

3. Gave supervisors an opportunity to discuss what they expected from their crewmembers.

When JetBlue announced the new leadership principles, it was part of the response to the Annual Speak-up Survey. Their first three words were, *"We are sorry."* JetBlue executive leadership listened, held themselves accountable, and took action.

Wait, wait, wait! Hold your horses for one minute! Are you telling me that setting expectations is a two-way street and we should communicate as such? Please see both the sarcasm and seriousness of the last three sentences. It's just as Dave Barger said ... "a radical approach to common sense!" And I'm saying it again because it's one of my favorite quotes and because it's so incredibly relevant in today's workplace. I hope you're thinking the same thing and are picturing times in your own work experience when common sense was thrown out the window. Those big "common-sense failures" alone could fill a book, but I recall a specific moment in my career wherein an executive leader said the following ... publicly: "If we're hiring the right people, they should know what to do in their job." Wait for it ... AAAAAAAAAAAHHHHHHH. That's me screaming and cringing and throwing punches at the air! I couldn't believe then, and still don't believe now, that someone with the privilege to lead could be so obtuse about how much our employees need and deserve from us. It's yet another example of being too smart for simple.

Making the Values Stick

Another key component of JetBlue's implementation of the five core values and five leadership principles is how they made them stick. Leadership involved current crewmembers in the hiring process for new crewmembers to ensure new hires fit within JetBlue's values and leadership principles. Crewmembers knew those values and principles well, as they were communicated often and embedded within JetBlue's performance management program. Within the hiring process, the company had what they termed the "BlueDart" program (employee referrals). The crewmember responsible for referring a candidate would be part of the screening of *that* candidate (peer screening their own referrals). This created a whole new meaning for staking one's own name to a candidate. JetBlue also found that it created great diversity in the candidate pool.

Leadership involved current crewmembers in the hiring process for new crewmembers to ensure new hires fit within JetBlue's values and leadership principles.

There's so much we can learn from leaders like Mike Barger, and I'm grateful for the time he spent chatting with me so I could share his insights with you. Let me leave you with several parting comments he made to me, because these gems of insights we should all pay attention to.

1. When done right, a company's core values and leadership principles get woven into the fabric of the company just as they have been with JetBlue.

2. Select a leadership team using simple yet meaningful questions like these:
    -   Do they have the right skill set?
    -   Do they have the right experience?
    -   Do they have the passion (enthusiasm) to achieve the goals?
    -   Do their personalities fit?

- Do they find a way to ensure every single crewmember is aligned with the vision, mission, and values of the team?

3. Common team-building mistakes leaders make include:
   - Not creating a specific common purpose.
   - Unclear roles and responsibilities.
   - Not changing the team composition when needed.

4. Common traits of a high-performing team:
   - Clarity on who's playing what role.
   - Understanding among team members that their individual roles are part of the team's overall success.
   - Mutual trust.
   - Open, transparent communication.

5. Regular interval health checks (what's going well on the team and what's not).

6. Discretionary effort. It's what sets companies apart. An extra 1, 2, or 3% from everyone adds up to make a difference.

Discretionary effort. It's what sets companies apart. An extra 1, 2, or 3% from everyone adds up to make a difference.

CHAPTER 5

The White House

A New Kind of Leadership Crucible

My heart was beating faster than normal as I was standing in the doorway of the curator's office in the Denver Museum of Nature and Science. Sitting at the curator's desk was President Barack Obama. Press Secretary Robert Gibbs was standing next to him and Vice President Joe Biden stood nearby. The room was cramped with a big desk, a small round table, a few chairs, bookcases, and our communications equipment sitting on a table along the wall. There were no windows. This was the curator's office, not messy, just stuffy. I stood at the doorway for what seemed like an eternity but, in reality, was only about 30 seconds as I waited for Vice President Biden, the White House photographer, and the President's assistant, Reggie Love, to exit the room.

Of course, my nerves were on high alert, but they calmed quickly when I entered the room and was only a few feet away from the desk where the President was sitting. He and Secretary Gibbs were bantering back and forth. F-Bomb this, F-Bomb that! Cursing like Sailors they were, and it put me at ease. In my head I thought, *"They sound just like me and my troops sometimes. They're normal people. Let's get his show on the road!"*

We got right down to business. There were three radio disc jockeys (DJs) waiting to do their interviews with the President. Using one of the military phones I had set up for the President in the office, I conferenced in one radio show at a time, along with the White House Director of Communications, and our audio visual master control office, and at the right time introduced the President to the DJ and gave the President the handset to conduct the interview. Each interview went off with precision and without issue. It was what we called Presidential Quality (i.e., nothing went wrong)!

This was February 17, 2009. President Obama had just been sworn in as the 44th President of the United States the month prior. This was also the day he signed into law the American Recovery and Reinvestment Act of 2009. I was leading the communications team onsite at the museum where the President signed the bill, sitting at a desk we had set up for him next to the podium on stage. After President Obama was finished on stage, he proceeded to the curator's office, which I had pretty much commandeered six days prior and had turned it into an office the President could use if he needed to. And as it turned out, on this day, he needed it.

WHCA

That event with President Obama was unquestionably one of the most exhilarating times of my life. AND I'M A REPUBLICAN! The President of the United States is the Commander in Chief, Chief Executive, and Head of State. Regardless of who is elected to office, the President must be able to carry out those three roles and have all the resources needed to do so ... and for a period of time, "those resources" included me.

I had the honor of serving for a total of 10 years with the White House Communications Agency (also known simply as WHCA, pronounced

"Wa-Ka") during two separate tours within my 20+ years on active duty in the Army. The final 7 ½ years of my Army career were spent as the Chief of HR Operations and Presidential Communications Officer, which included time with President George W. Bush and President Barack Obama.

For context, WHCA is an organization that falls under the hierarchy of the White House Military Office (WHMO), which is led by a political appointee of the President. WHCA provides global information services to the President, Vice President, Executive Office of the President, and United States Secret Service, ensuring the ability of the White House to communicate anywhere, anytime, and by any means to anyone![1]

The White House Military Office also includes the Presidential Airlift Group, White House Medical Unit, Camp David, Marine Helicopter Squadron One, Presidential Food Service, and the White House Transportation Agency. Most Americans likely presume that some of these functions are performed by civilian, at-will employees, but they're actually all military units. Inside WHCA alone, there are approximately 1,000 White House "staffers" who are active duty members of the Armed Forces, and significantly more active duty members of the Armed Forces (from other agencies and offices) supporting the White House every day.

Before we get in to some more stories, I want to highlight why these Presidential stories are important, relevant, and supportive of the subtitle of this book: "Leading Organizations to Values-Based Results." The political environment of the United States continues to get more and more polarizing from one President to the next, especially as administrations change from one political party to the other. Just think about the different personalities and leadership styles of

---

[1]   https://www.disa.mil/careers/WHCA-Recruitment

President Clinton, President Bush, President Obama, and President Trump. I'm not sure that even the most creative fiction authors of our time could create the personas of these four presidents if they tried! In Washington and at the ballot box, we often have one party against the other, no matter what the issue. And, as of the writing of this book, there's almost no civil debate. Even mainstream media outlets are tilting left or right, and spinning stories and crafting narratives in a way that goes beyond (or below) just reporting the news.

So how, then, do the men and women directly supporting the White House — people whose jobs don't change as administrations change but who all have their own personal political opinions and express them in the voting booth — continue to perform at the highest levels possible? Answer: They live, breathe, and behave in accordance with a set of core values that puts mission before self.

For me, it was the Army values and the values of WHCA and WHMO. WHCA's tagline is "The Voice of the President." It doesn't say the voice of President Clinton, or Bush, or Obama, or Trump. No name need be added.

Imagine that you're a loyal, committed Democrat and you hold a permanent government position in the Executive Office of the President (EOP). You're a careerist and have no plans on finding a new job just because President Bush, President Trump, or another Republican President is in office and could get reelected for yet another term. What behaviors do you put on display every day? Answer: You demonstrate respect for the Office of the President and your co-workers, as well as a real display of Selfless Service.

There are literally several thousand government employees and military Service members in organizations directly supporting the President, Vice President, First Lady, and White House in general. If they can all behave at this level in a manner that's aligned with their organization's core values, just think what a company could do in corporate America if they had thousands of employees doing the same.

If thousands of government employees and military Service members can all behave at this level in a manner that's aligned with their organization's core values, just think what a company could do in corporate America if they had thousands of employees doing the same.

It was a privilege and honor to serve alongside my fellow teammates at the White House Communications Agency. Together, we provided the President with the highest quality communications as possible. We did it with no rehearsals, with tight timelines, and always with determination to be the best of the best. And I learned a great deal about values-based leadership along the way.

President Bush – #43

My very first event as a Presidential Communications Officer (PCO) was at Arlington National Cemetery on Memorial Day, May 28, 2007. I was just finishing my PCO training and this was the event where I had the opportunity to shadow another PCO before being assigned to represent our agency as the communications team leader for a POTUS (President of the United States) event. What an incredible event to have as the first. To be part of Memorial Day where President Bush gave remarks about the importance of the day and laid a wreath at the Tomb of the Unknown Soldier, all within the bounds of Arlington National Cemetery where thousands of our nation's warriors lie in rest .... Well, it was nothing less than amazing. What a day!

At the Memorial Day event, the First Lady, the Chairman of the Joint Chiefs, several Cabinet members, and several Congressional members were in attendance. If I was going to do well as a PCO, I had to quickly figure out how to not only get past the "shock and awe" of being in close proximity to the President and other high-profile people, but also how to lead teams in this zero-defect environment.

If I was going to do well as a PCO, I had to quickly figure out how to not only get past the "shock and awe" of being in close proximity to the President and other high-profile people, but also how to lead teams in this zero-defect environment.

My Check Ride

After shadowing the PCO on Memorial Day and shortly after finishing training, I had my "check ride" to become officially qualified to lead in-town events (i.e., events within the Washington, DC, metro area). Check ride was a term we used to identify the event the PCO was being graded upon by another already-qualified PCO. I was assigned as the PCO for an event President Bush was to attend at the State Department headquarters. Condoleezza Rice was the Secretary of State at the time.

The State Department headquarters is a typical government building full of security and protocol. I always found it to be very interesting to learn, execute, and accomplish the mission within a slew of different environments, all dependent on the location of the event. One thing WHCA operations was very good at was keeping checklists up to date, documenting historical information from previous trips, and communicating with the PCO in the field. We were constantly learning and perfecting our practices. These checklists and other resources made it seamless for the team to quickly adapt to different operational environments.

TIP

Want to guide employees to a specific set of behaviors aligned with the company's core values? Create a set of standards (e.g., checklists, process diagrams, mind maps, and workstreams) for all to follow. Whether you work at a start-up company or a Fortune 500 company, an appropriate level of structure and process will help drive desirable behaviors.

WHCA is a military unit and, as it goes with any military unit, a unit member's appearance is subject to a set of standards. For WHCA, this meant business attire. For me, it meant a traditional, pressed suit and tie. Even while setting up at the State Department in the week leading up to President Bush arriving for his event, I was in suit and tie getting communication/phone lines installed, sometimes even crawling around on my hands and knees to get the lines where I needed them.

On the day of the event (i.e., game day), the team is all business. Arrive early, get the radio infrastructure ready to go, get the U.S. Secret Service (USSS) agents radioed up, and get set for the POTUS arrival. For my check ride, I headed to the arrival point as soon as I heard the voice in my earpiece say that POTUS was getting in the limo and the motorcade was about the leave the White House. I stood at the arrival point, along with the onsite USSS and White House staff leads, as well as Secretary Rice, waiting for President Bush to arrive. It's quite a moment when the limo pulls up and the USSS agents from the trail vehicle (these agents are called the Presidential Protective Detail or PPD) pull in behind and all jump out to create a human bubble around the President. It's like an incredibly well-oiled machine, operating at full capacity and high speed. The PPD agents to the USSS are like the Special Forces are to the Army ... elite!

Mitt Romney's House

Park City, Utah. Up on the mountainside, just below the area's luxury ski resorts, sit some of the most beautiful log-cabin style mansions I'd ever seen in one place. Mitt Romney and his family owned one of them and it was grand, to say the least. Instead of having deer in the yard, like I'm used to seeing on the East Coast, this area had moose in the yard. They're gigantic animals!

This trip had multiple event sites between Salt Lake City and Park City. The team was led by U.S. Navy Chief Warrant Officer Greg Wagner (now retired). He oversaw the entire operation and he assigned me to handle the Republican National Committee (RNC) evening fundraiser that was being held at Mitt Romney's house. Greg displayed all the best leadership traits one could ask for. He communicated expectations of the team and the team was aware of what we could expect of Greg. Leading a team of high performers comes with the highest expectations of the leader. Greg lived up to them all.

Leading a team of high performers comes with the highest expectations of the leader.

The trip was in the off-season for the ski resorts. No snow and low occupancy. We had the best accommodations at the Stein Eriksen Lodge one could ask for. I even had a full-size hot tub on the balcony of my room, overlooking the slopes. And yes, regardless of how late it was when I got back to my room each night, I sat in that hot tub before calling it a day. This place even had a Lexus convertible sports coupe that guests could check out and tool around town in. And yes, when the trip was done, we had one night before flying back to DC, so Greg and I reserved the car and drove it to dinner and did a little sightseeing in Park City.

On the first morning after arriving in Park City, we did a walk-through of the Romney log mansion. I had my radio and satellite lead, as well as my audio-visual lead, with me. Together with the White House Staff and USSS leads, we were introduced to Mrs. Romney and she gave us a tour of the entire house to kick things off. She was very kind and very accommodating, and incredibly gracious about the fact that we were basically taking over her home for the next six days! Believe it or not, Mitt was outside trimming trees near the deck and scaring off a momma moose and her not-so-little baby. We completed our onsite visit and went right to work getting everything prepped for game day.

Early in the morning on game day, before President Bush arrived at the Salt Lake City airport, I had the honor of checking all the communications equipment in the President's limo. After getting permission from the highly skilled USSS agent assigned to drive the limo, he started the engine and I opened the incredibly heavy and thick door to access where the President would sit when he got in. Folks, these are no ordinary doors. Accidentally shut that door on a body part and bones will be crushed!

I sat in the President's seat (nice car, by the way) and made sure the equipment we were responsible for was working as it should. After exiting the limo, I walked back to the operations site, which the team had set up at the airport, and I was later told by the team that the news station got me on camera and the rest of the team had seen me on TV. Not good for me, as it was common practice that anyone caught on TV buys the beer!

I headed back to Park City and to the Romney house to go through my game-day checklist with the team and to ensure we were ready for President Bush's arrival later in the evening. The event was a private fundraiser for about 70 guests and was closed to the press. The RNC set up a table at the entrance to the house and collected guest donations (large ones) prior to letting guests into the house. It was pretty cool to watch people walk down the driveway and line up to write a check. The caterers had set up in the garage and any good caterer always has a little extra food, so suffice it to say that the WHCA team ate well that night.

My only run-in with Mitt Romney himself was during one of my trips through the garage. It was still an hour or so before the President's arrival, and I had passed through the open garage doors checking on things (kind of like making rounds). As I turned to come back into the garage, down comes one of the garage doors toward my head. I yelled, "Hey, stop the door!" Right as the door stopped on its track, Senator Romney popped out with eyes wide open and apologized profusely for hitting the button and almost knocking me out. Nice guy for sure, but dangerous with a garage door opener!

Even though the event was closed to the press, we still had a duty to record the President's remarks to the guests. We were set up on a stairway landing that overlooked the Romney's family room where the guests were seated, and the President was talking and answering questions. This was the first closed press event I had ever attended with President Bush. In that hour or so, I witnessed the President speak and respond like never before. There was no prepared speech. His remarks were off the cuff, and guests were asking questions on nearly every current topic of the day. He addressed questions about the war in Iraq and Afghanistan, about terrorism, about the economy, and on policies and trends related to immigration and more. President Bush took those questions like a champ. His responses were deep. They were filled with critical thought. It seemed genuine and passionate. Not a stump speech or prepared remarks from a speech writer. The exact thought in my head as I listened, "The whole *country* needs to hear this, not just the 70 guests in the room and those of us working the event." When a leader stands, speaks, and delivers with care, passion, and competence, it's received with genuine trust and confidence in return.

Chicago in the Winter

My trip to Chicago was led by Lieutenant Colonel Jim Henderson. Jim was an Air Force officer and he had two Army Warrant Officers leading event sites on this trip, me and Wayne Pohl. We may have drove the Colonel a little crazy on this trip with all our questions, but that's what good Warrant Officers do, ask lots of questions to ensure we get it right and then teach it to others. All three of us have long since retired and there's much respect for those days in Chicago.

It was wintertime. Unless you like bitter cold temperatures, extreme ice like wind gusts, and a ton of snow, going on a POTUS trip to Chicago in the middle of winter didn't seem like such a great idea. But nonetheless, it wasn't our job to second guess the President's schedule. It was our job to execute it, anytime of the day at any place in the world. So off to Chicago we went.

We arrived in downtown at our hotel in the afternoon. The truck full of our equipment was waiting on us and we got at it. Was it snowing? Dumb question. Of course it was snowing ... hard. Folks, the President was arriving in 7 days and there's no such thing as a snow day, so we had to get to work. I went up on the roof of the hotel with the satellite team to lend a hand setting things up. There had to be almost two feet of snow on the roof and it was pretty much stacked that high on the ledge, where we had to drop the cable over the side and guide it to the window of one of our office setups.

I think I was the highest-ranking person on the roof and the whole thing was ripe with danger. I've jumped out of airplanes, hung about a 100 feet below a helicopter on a steel cable and flown around so the pilots could practice extraction techniques, bungee jumped, and a few other high risk activities, but nothing presented the risk I was seeing while 20 floors above the street on the snow packed roof of this Chicago hotel. We huddled on the roof, quickly talked through a risk assessment, and as a team, figured out the right way (i.e. the safest way) to get the satellite dish set up and the cable over the ledge without anyone falling. You can guess what happens when you free fall from 20 floors up. Risk assessment 101...probability the event will happen paired against the probability of the worst possible outcome, death.

Leaders have a duty to watch out for their people. Duty is a core value of leadership (and one of the seven Army values to which I hold myself accountable). Even if it doesn't come with a level of risk, like falling off a building, being cognizant of what your people are doing and the risks associated therein, followed by taking steps to reduce risk as much as possible is a key characteristic of a good leader. The point here is to illustrate the more you're tied into the behaviors surrounding your core values, the better the results you'll get.

My event site this week in Chicago was in one of the city's elementary schools. President Bush was scheduled to come in, visit a couple classrooms, and then give remarks in the gymnasium with a few classes of children in attendance. The event went off as planned and there wasn't any pomp and circumstance associated with it, but in my opinion, the White House staff lead made a big fubar during the day President Bush was in the school. Each classroom had a solid door entrance with a window next to it. You could see in the classroom and the kids could see out, but not on this day. The staff lead had all the classrooms, except the two the President was visiting, cover the entire window next to the door with black construction paper. I guess they thought chaos would ensue and there'd be little kid pileups inside the classrooms as they all tried to get a peek at President Bush walking down the hallway!

Walter Reed Army Medical Center – Respect in Action

The wars in Iraq and Afghanistan have been riddled with the enemy's favorite weapon, the improvised explosive device (IED). IEDs have caused thousands of deaths and even more injuries, many of which resulted in the loss of limbs. The amputee and rehabilitation areas of Walter Reed Army Medical Center have seen a large number of these troops and their families come through their doors. May God bless all the troops, their families, and the entire staff at Walter Reed for helping our members of the Armed Forces recover from the tragedies they faced.

Before the Walter Reed Army Medical Center was transitioned to the Walter Reed National Medical Center at Naval Support Activity in Bethesda, Maryland, I had the opportunity as the PCO of a very special event with President Bush. I get choked up just thinking about writing this.

No big setup was needed. No podium or teleprompters. No special lighting. This was a day President Bush visited the amputee floor and awarded several Purple Hearts to unexpecting troops. Walter Reed is a military installation and while the President was on the amputee floor, he didn't have quite the entourage following along as usual. It only included a half dozen folks or so and I was privileged to be one of them. The President went from room to room, every one of them, saying hello and talking for a couple minutes with the troop and his or her family. Those to whom he was presenting the Purple Heart experienced an impromptu awards ceremony, which left witnesses and participants full of emotion.

The President's Military Aide (Mil-Aide) handed me the nuclear football before entering the room of the Soldier receiving the Purple Heart. As quick as the thought went through my mind that, "Holy cow, I'm holding the football," the Mil-Aide stood next to the hospital bed and read the award citation as President Bush pinned the Purple Heart medal to the Soldier's chest. I was looking in from just outside the room, doing my best to be inconspicuous, as this was a very special moment between two people, the Commander-in-Chief and his Soldier!

New Jersey with President Obama – #44

I had some anxiety built up for this trip to New Jersey as the PCO for an event with President Obama. My anxiety didn't have anything to do with the President, but was related to the Lieutenant Colonel leading the trip, Chris Roth. I had never traveled on POTUS trips with Chris before. Around our headquarters office, he was known to be a bit of a hard ass. I had worked with Chris on numerous things around the office not related to POTUS events and found him to have high expectations of others, but he also delivered in return. The anxiety I was feeling was simply coming from the depths of the unknown and in the end, it was Chris — through his actions, behaviors, and incredible leadership — who put my fears to rest.

When the team arrived in New Jersey, we got right to work just as with any other POTUS trip. A very high level of communication from Chris started immediately. The entire team was well informed and charged to attend to their piece of the puzzle. What set me at ease from the start was the level of trust and confidence Chris showed in me. He checked on me, asked if I had the resources I needed, asked my opinion about the event site, and even took time to mentor me on various aspects of my role as a PCO. This guy, a hard ass? No way. He's a leader in every way we desire leaders to be. There wasn't a single person on the team who didn't think that. Loyalty to the team and a sense of duty beyond reproach. We all showed Chris the highest level of respect possible, not because of his rank but because of his leadership.

One day when Chris was at the event site with me, he noticed that my HR boss back at the headquarters office had called me several times. Chris pulled me aside and asked if I needed him to give the boss a call and set him straight ... to help him get his mind in the right place, if you will. He would let him know I had a job to do for President Obama, who happened to rank a little higher on the priority list, and to stop calling me or we'd have a problem. That's the kind of leader Chris is. He has your back ... always!

President Obama came into town and we were ready. As usual, the event concluded with no issues. This was a pretty cool event held in an amphitheater that seated about 6,000 people. Literally two days before the President arrived, we were working the event site while they were setting up for a Twisted Sister concert the night before the President took the stage to speak. Quite the combo of events that week in New Jersey!

The Black-Tie Event

This was one of my favorite events from my years of service to the White House. The Congressional Hispanic Caucus held a black-tie event at the Walter E. Washington Convention Center, DC, and Chief Warrant Officer Donzell Johnson (RIP, Brother) was assigned this event as his qualification check ride. I had the honor to be the check ride officer.

The team had tuxedo measurements on file with a local DC formal-wear shop and we had our orders placed, fittings done, and picked up our attire for the big event. Our responsibilities and requirements were the same as for any other event, only we had to get dressed up like the attendees and, more specifically, like President Obama would. It was fun and we fit in backstage, where we always were for POTUS events.

The evening was going really well. Donzell and I, along with a couple other event participants, were standing backstage when we saw her. Donzell and I looked at each other and were like, *"Could it really be her?"* She was wearing a long black dress, high heels, and was walking toward us. We kept looking at each other, then back at her, then at each other until she was close enough to confirm her identity. Sure enough, we were in the presence of Eva Longoria. Wow! It was the superstar actress well known for her role the hit TV show *Desperate Housewives*. She was with her then-NBA player husband, Tony Parker. As much as we would have liked to strike up a conversation, that wasn't the protocol. We kept our composure, remained professional, and just took in the moment for what it was. But I'll tell you, if someone would have tapped me on the shoulder at that precise moment and asked where President Obama was, I would have said, "Who?"

The West Wing

As much fun as I had giving family and friends tours of the West Wing, it really functions just like a government office building. The West Wing and East Wing are part of the White House and if it wasn't for our nation's history, coupled with all the activity that's taken place in the West Wing — and the fact that it's next to impossible to get in — there wouldn't be much to see or talk about. As buildings themselves go, the Mall in DC is filled with more exquisite ones than the West Wing. But nonetheless, it's "the what and the who" that make it so intriguing.

Whenever I was giving a tour of the West Wing, which included the Rose Garden and the Press Briefing Room, it was always a big deal for my guests, and I did my best to be a good tour guide. I had several guests who had the opportunity to meet both White House Chief of Staff Rahm Emanuel and Press Secretary Robert Gibbs, both of whom purposely came out of their offices to say hello. As for my guests, the engagement made their day!

It's Possible to Achieve Astonishing Results

Many people have written books about their time serving at the White House — about their interactions with one President or another, and about all they learned and saw and accomplished. All have their stories and they're fun to read. My decade in the White House was filled with leadership lessons from up, down, and across the organization. I learned and I grew, and I came away knowing that, with great leadership and a strong commitment to a shared set of core values, the results can be astonishing. The men and women of the White House Military Office put their values on display every day and never falter. Those values put them above political mantra and put the mission before self. Be better, know better, and do better!

Letters from the Top

Serving inside the White House was truly an honor. I suspect that I'll be sharing the stories and applying the lessons I learned — there in those hallowed halls and around the nation in support of President Bush and President Obama — for the rest of my career and my life.

When I look back on that decade, my overwhelming feeling is one of gratitude.

CHIEF OF STAFF TO THE PRESIDENT

THE WHITE HOUSE

December 15, 2006

Chief Warrant Officer Robert E. Brabo, USA
White House Communications Agency
The White House
East Wing, 2nd Floor

Dear Bo:

Earlier this year, the President reminded us that "the history of America is one of constant renewal. And each generation has a responsibility to write a new chapter in the unfinished story of freedom." As we approach the New Year, I want to thank you for your contribution to this continuing story.

During this time of consequence, you are helping the President to strengthen our Nation's economy, protect the American people, and spread freedom around the world. The President knows that your service requires substantial sacrifice, from your family as well as from you. As you spend time at home over the holidays, please extend my gratitude to those whose support makes your service here at the White House possible.

I wish you a joyful holiday season and all the best in the New Year. It is a privilege serving with you.

Sincerely,

Joshua B. Bolten

CHIEF OF STAFF TO THE PRESIDENT

THE WHITE HOUSE

December 6, 2010

Chief Warrant Officer Robert E. Brabo II
White House Military Office
Washington, D.C.

Dear Bo:

In this year's State of the Union address, the President said, "It's time the American people get a Government that matches their decency; that embodies their strength." As the year draws to a close, I want to thank you for your hard work and dedication toward achieving this vision.

Every day, through difficult tasks and long hours, you have been a reflection of those ideals as well. Your hard work does not go unnoticed. With your help, we have made great progress on many of the issues that face our Nation. And, as we look ahead, your contributions will again prove vital in helping the President restore our economy, preserve our security, and build a better future for all Americans. As you gather with your family this holiday season, please know the President and I are grateful for all that you do.

We send our best wishes to you and your loved ones, and we look forward to serving with you in the New Year.

Sincerely,

Peter M. Rouse

CHIEF OF STAFF TO THE PRESIDENT

THE WHITE HOUSE

December 14, 2011

Chief Warrant Officer Robert E. Brabo II
White House Military Office - WHCA
Washington, D.C.

Dear Bo:

As I reflect upon this past year, I am incredibly grateful for your commitment to the President and to the American people. The countless hours you have worked and many sacrifices you and your family have made exemplify the true meaning of public service.

In a speech in Tucson, Arizona, at the beginning of this year, President Obama said, "we should do everything we can to make sure this country lives up to our children's expectations." Your efforts every day are moving the country toward this ideal.

As we enjoy the holiday season, we remain mindful of our fellow Americans who are struggling to make ends meet and to provide for their families. Your work this year has shown that you share the President's tireless commitment to finding solutions to our Nation's many challenges, and I am confident that together we will continue to make progress for the American people in the new year.

On behalf of the President, I wish you and your loved ones a holiday season filled with joy and peace, and I look forward to our continued service together.

Sincerely,

William M. Daley

CHIEF OF STAFF TO THE PRESIDENT

THE WHITE HOUSE

December 7, 2012

Chief Warrant Officer Three Robert E. Brabo II, USA
White House Military Office - WHCA
Washington, D.C.

Dear Bo:

With the holiday season upon us, I want to take a moment to thank you for your tremendous work on behalf of the President.

At times, the demands of our jobs may seem endless, and the day-to-day accomplishments may be taken for granted. This past year brought its share of enormous and complex challenges across our desks, and I am proud of you and your work to respond—both individually and collectively—to our country's needs.

There remains much work to do as we implement the President's vision for a strong middle class, an economy built to last, and a safer, more peaceful world. I am confident that, together, we can build on the progress of the last four years and continue to move our Nation forward towards a more prosperous future.

As we take time over the holidays to be with loved ones, I hope you know how grateful I am for all of the sacrifices you and your family have made in order to serve the President and the American people.

Sincerely,

Jack Lew

CHAPTER 6

Resilience and Humanity

Insights from Rachel Noble, Mental Health Researcher at Johns Hopkins University and Director of INOVA Women's Behavioral Health

Rachel Noble is many things. She's a good friend, colleague, mental health professional, volunteer, freelance writer, conference speaker, researcher, and selfless leader. Rachel holds a graduate degree in Mental Health Counseling from The Johns Hopkins University and an undergraduate degree in Medical Ethics from George Mason University. She's the Director of INOVA Women's Behavioral Health and she's the President of the Allay Foundation, where she helps provide mental healthcare for low-income moms struggling with maternal mental illness. Rachel is one of the rock stars of mental health!

Wherever she goes, Rachel inspires and supports those around her. Aside from the countless number of patients Rachel has helped over the years, she's taken the active internal role of executive coach in every organization she's worked in. In my own experience working with Rachel, I would say because of her welcoming character, vast skillset and experience, and most importantly her willingness to listen, she's often drawn into workplace coaching whether she wants to be or not. I met Rachel at Advantia Health, where I was the Vice

President of Human Resources and she was the Director of Mental Wellness, and I was always dragging her into the office for regular coaching sessions. I'll say this and then move on ... In my 26+ years in the Army, the phrase "physical and mental toughness" was just as common as "technical and tactical proficiency" was. Both phrases used in gauging a Soldier's performance. Mental toughness is the mind's ability to overcome fear, stress, anxiety, fatigue, perform critical thought, make tough decisions in times of distress or real crisis, and more. Mental toughness is where personal courage — one of the Army's core values — comes from. Rachel's counsel in this regard absolutely raised the bar of my own mental toughness, for which I am forever grateful.

Mental Fitness for Leaders

I wish I didn't have to remind anyone, but it's important that we don't mistake mental health for mental illness. We all have "mental health" needs, and some of us have mental illness, just as we all have physical health needs but may or may not be suffering from a physical illness. Mental health is just as critical to our overall health as physical fitness is, and it's vital to our leadership abilities as well. As a society, we need to work on ridding the world of the stigma associated with regular engagement with a mental health professional like Rachel, especially within our active duty military and Veteran communities.

I must note that Rachel's work throughout her distinguished career has been on the international stage across multiple continents. As I listened to Rachel talk about her experiences while she was availing herself for the interviews I conducted while writing this book, I very much realized that what you'll read below comes from the perspective of simply being human. Being mentally "fit" as leaders, according to Rachel, requires attention to five key areas, and these areas are universally applicable — regardless of the kind of organization in which you lead and irrespective of your own personal or professional background. We all have stimuli bombarding our minds every moment of every day and we respond (i.e., behave) in a multitude of ways. And as I believe that behavior over time by many people in an organization creates a culture, and that the culture (and the behaviors) reflect either shared or diverging sets of values, I was fascinated to hear Rachel's take on the areas of mental health that can influence workplace behaviors.

These are the five specific mental health areas that Rachel says leaders should be aware of and keen to action on:

1. Burnout to Resiliency

2. Paradigm Shift

3. Measuring Outcomes

4. Rewards

5. Fear

Have you ever felt like you were truly at your wits end? Convinced that your energy to continue at the same pace and quality of work has been fully depleted? If yes, you're facing burnout. I'm sure many of us have had long workdays, worked multiple jobs to make a living, or have gone days without sleep facing the perils of combat or the stressors of civilian life. It feels like the marathon that doesn't end. The marathon, 26.2 miles, is a good analogy here. I've run a dozen half marathons but never a full one and when I speak to those who have, they all say the same thing. When they hit the 18-mile mark or so, the run changes from a physical one to a mental one. They're burned out, both physically and mentally. The body is telling the mind it's done, and the mind agrees. For the runner to get through the next 8.2 miles, he or she *must* transition their mind from burnout to resiliency, harnessing the power to recover from, ignore, or overcome adversity.

Have you ever felt like you were truly at your wits end? Convinced that your energy to continue at the same pace and quality of work has been fully depleted? If yes, you're facing burnout.

Rachel's current work at INOVA has her working on this very issue as it pertains to physicians. Fascinating work. Imagine you're a doctor seeing 25 to 30 patients during the day and having to pull call at the hospital at night and on the weekends. What do you think would be a reasonable schedule? Physicians will tell you a reasonable call schedule would be something between 1 in every 4th to 6th weekday and 1 in every 4th to 6th weekend. Every 6th is great, but anything less than every 4th is a sign of trouble. You can see where a healthcare organization with a shortage of physicians could be demanding shifts from their clinicians that are destined to lead to burnout. Leaders have to pay attention to what's taking place across their organizations to identify the potential for burnout and address it head-on.

How do you change from mental burnout to mental resiliency? Train, train, and train some more. In the Army we call it "train as you fight." You don't train for a marathon by running 10 miles once or twice and then sign-up for a race and think you'll make it 26.2 miles. Start with a self-assessment and develop a realistic training plan that will take you to your limits. I'm not a research doctor or scientist, but I've read enough of their studies to know the brain needs training and exercise to be healthy, strong, and resilient. But it also needs rest … you can't run a marathon every day without one day being your last.

Rachel explains that people want to be listened to. Wow! Another "wait a minute, hold your horses" kind of moment. I absolutely love this because it sounds off the warning sirens that leaders fail big and often at the most critical part of communication ... listening. Think back to the physicians referred to moments ago. Now imagine they're working five days a week, seeing 125 to 130 patients in the office each week, and pulling call every other weeknight and every other weekend (1 in 2) and it's been like that for months. They have addressed the issue with leadership over and over, to include referencing the fact that they're getting burned out. An analogy, yes, but it's happening (particularly with medical residents). Studies show that physicians have among the highest suicide rate of any single profession in the United States. There aren't enough people listening and our physicians keep getting pushed to the edge.

Leaders fail big and often at the most critical part of communication ... listening.

On a positive note, when leaders do listen, as Mike Barger and the entire leadership team did at JetBlue, we see real change and results from their actions.

It's Lonely (and Scary) at the Top: Fear and Leadership

Given the overarching theme of this book and my passion for leading organizations to values-based results, I asked Rachel why she thinks some company leaders aren't able to execute upon the very values they say they believe in. Why would any leader *not* choose to live and breathe (i.e., to align their everyday workplace behaviors to) their core values and drive the same behaviors up and down the organization to generate profound results. Her answer? Fear!

"People are so afraid of doing it wrong, so they don't do anything. Fear becomes paralyzing." – Rachel Noble.

I mentioned earlier that it took me about an hour to craft and send a single email to Mike Barger. Had I not had Rachel's counsel and coaching in my head I may have never sent the email at all. But I did. I had the mental tools to work through it. I was able to put a measurement on the outcome (25% chance of getting a yes and nothing lost if I get a no) and the actual decision to send the email — once I got myself in the right mindset — was quick and easy.

After talking with Rachel, I truly believe that fear or worry is the one thing preventing way too many corporate executives from achieving the best possible results for their companies. Fear of failure, fear of getting fired, fear of losing stockholder value, fear of not being liked by their employees. Despite the fact that most current and aspiring leaders have heard story after story about wildly successful leaders having failed hard and failed often before they got it right, most leaders are still held back by fear. If even one person paralyzed by fear reads this book and uses something they read to gain momentum to beat down fear at the door, I will stand up and cheer. Fear stands between us and our most important leadership opportunities. I was scared the first time I jumped out of an airplane; there was fear when I took a Special Ops assignment in the Army; I was worried about what awaited me at the White House and in every organization where I've worked. But fear is the enemy. I think about the Army's value of Personal Courage and I know that it can be hard to muster it up. But I know you can do it! And in many ways, your employees and stakeholders are counting on you to do it.

Despite the fact that most current and aspiring leaders have heard story after story about wildly successful leaders having failed hard and failed often before they got it right, most leaders are still held back by fear.

Measure, Reward, and Keep Going

Rachel has taught me a great deal about building and maintaining the mind of a leader, and about taking care of my mental health and the mental health of those around me. She believes that a critical step in mental health is having the ability to measure outcomes. In medicine, clinicians constantly strive to practice in an "evidence-based" way, not just making diagnoses and treatment plans based on hunches, but advising and treating their patients based on what the *evidence* suggests is actually working. You don't have to be a doctor to care about evidence-based practice; in fact, leading people and projects in any industry should be about what works ... what generates positive outcomes. When we behave in certain ways (hopefully in alignment with our core values!) and produce an item of measure, we can see the results. It's information we can grab on to and do something about. Whether that's staying on the same course or having to change course, we have evidence guiding us in the right direction. Evidence creates confidence, and confidence can be a powerful deterrent to fear and even burnout.

So, be sure to measure the outcomes of your practices at work, especially your leadership behaviors and the admirable behaviors of others. And then *reward* that behavior. Rachel is passionate about the importance of recognizing and rewarding people when they make positive changes in their behavior. We must take time to appreciate the "little steps" (i.e., achieving the smaller goals along the journey), which comes right back to behaviors in the workplace. Do you as a leader, or your company, celebrate the small things as they occur or blow right by them because they're part of the job? Sometimes a pat on the back, a high-five, a fist bump, or taking someone to lunch for a job well done is more mentally monumental than a cash bonus at the end of the year.

Sometimes a pat on the back, a high-five, a fist bump, or taking someone to lunch for a job well done is more mentally monumental than a cash bonus at the end of the year.

CHAPTER 7

The Boardroom

Leadership Reflections from Corporate America

From the battlefield ... to the White House ... to the boardroom. I've worked in many places and have honed my skills in different types of leadership crucibles. I am literally "battle-tested," have been challenged to deliver zero-defect "Presidential Results," and now operate from the vantage point of the corporate C-suite.

I'm guessing that you, too, have worked in a business — big or small — that operates within a competitive industry, that has sometimes overwhelming "people issues" or so-called "politics," that struggles with hierarchies and bureaucracy and proverbial "red tape," and that has shown you what good (and bad!) leadership looks like.

The Boardroom IS Corporate America

Often called Corporate America, we could even call it "Civilian America" — referring to anyone outside of the military and government. And it was important to me that this book addresses leadership in various environments because leaders are prone to "different strokes for different folks," meaning that Military Service Members, Government Employees, and then Civilian America all play by a different set of rules. There are Federal, State, and Local laws written and implemented for Civilian America that don't apply to their own government employees. There is a completely separate justice system for military service members called "The Uniform Code of Military Justice." And there are different overtime rules for the government contractor (non-government employee) who sits in the cubicle right next to the government employee supporting the same government agency.

Like it or not, there are external forces that have an impact on people as they go to work every day. We don't make the rules, but we have to live by them. How we behave in these various environments (i.e., our Values; or our B+t=V) quickly forms our identity in the workplace and when combined with our coworkers, determines the culture and propensity to achieve desired results ((B+t)*En=C).

The stories that follow are mine. Individual and company names have been left out on purpose. These stories are not meant to disparage or give praise. Put yourself in the story and think about the impact the behaviors displayed would have on you, on the team, and on the company.

Paranoia

Definition: baseless or excessive suspicion of the motives of others.

There I was one afternoon, sitting in my office working away. I had an urge for a cup of coffee ... a regular afternoon occurrence for me ... and as I exited my office, I saw the CEO standing outside of another office a few doors down and with his head/ear up against the door. There was a meeting taking place behind the closed door and he was eavesdropping. He saw me and it was evident that I saw him. He walked away from the door toward me and I stopped him. I had too much leadership experience to *not* address the situation (respect, duty, personal courage all come to mind). No disparagement, no condemnation, no judgement, just a quick subdued pep-talk in the hallway ... "You are the CEO, the leader of this company. Own it and sit in any meeting you'd like. Share your expertise and allow others to share theirs. Build trust and confidence in each other." He was exercising his curiosity and power in precisely the wrong way, when he had every right or opportunity to participate differently, and with more honor.

While I was surprised to see him with his ear against a door, I understood why he might have done it. There is immense pressure at the top and people behave differently based on a multitude of factors. Background, upbringing, experience, self-confidence, competence, education, and the list goes on. I'm not a mental health professional, but I am a servant leader and I know that humiliating someone is not a tactic that generates desired results, nor is it a behavior that would exemplify great leadership. So my natural inclination was not to shame the CEO for what I'd "caught" him doing. I knew, however, that I could try to help him see the situation differently, for the benefit of all.

In small business, it's common for margins to be tight, cash to be tight, and lines of credit often a must-have in order to make payroll. Not to mention, the constant pressure for the sales or business development team to keep the pedal to the metal. Competition is fierce and a small business can be out of business quicker than they got into it. I get it. It's stressful and lonely and scary at the top. As such, there's no shame in being a paranoid leader or being afraid of going out of business. The key is recognizing when the paranoia or fear are driving less than admirable behaviors so you can accept positive critique, develop a sound strategy, and then act on it.

TIP

Take time to care, and take care to show it. In my opinion, which is not unique, caring about others is the most critical aspect of leadership. If you don't care — more importantly if you don't *demonstrate* that you care — influencing and motivating others to do what you want them to is superficial at best.

Exponential Growth

I've learned a lot by being inside organizations in "growth mode." When a small business experiences exponential growth, in this case from fewer than 200 employees to more than 900 employees in less than two years across multiple states, the demands on the corporate support teams can be brutal. New people arrive and must get ramped up as quickly as possible. Even though managers, HR, and peers might do their best to explain the fast pace during the hiring process, it's usually not until you're in such an environment that it can be truly appreciated.

I was walking down the hall one day headed to my office, which was next to the acquisition team's office, and I saw the CEO sitting with one of our finance analysts. Together, they were reviewing pro-forma financial statements for a new deal being worked on. I would often see the CFO doing this as well — sitting at conference tables and across the desks of others, helping to solve problems with people at every level of the organization. C-Suite engagement in this type of environment was consistent, always respectful, and drove the team to achieve the growth the company was experiencing. It was a good example of selfless service, another Army value I hold dear.

Don't get me wrong. These rapid-growth environments come with a slew of other challenges and people are on edge. It's not all excitement during "scale-up." It's like your senses are at a heightened stage all the time and events requiring crisis management or course correction, like Mike Barger describes in the foreword to this book, are ever prevalent.

Indeed, the pressure at the top is immense. Even when personal and corporate values seem to be well aligned and the company is achieving significant results, people are not perfect and tend to slip up now and then. The same CEO in this rapidly expanding company, the one who employees appreciated for his willingness to sit side-by-side with them, had a day when the pressure won. Yelling erupted up and down the hallway, and startled our senses. This was such an uncommon behavior from the CEO that it caused all those within earshot to start the rumor mill about what could have caused his outburst.

I couldn't let that linger. I helped lead a rapid response action plan, got the facts in order, and then got the details to the employees to calm fears and put a stop to the rumors. I was determined to stop the behavior (or the emulation of it by others), discourage eruption over an unknown, teach employees to seek facts instead of gossip, and inspire my colleagues to remember the values we embody and got us where we are.

Social Responsibility

I've always admired organizations that go above and beyond to "do good" in the greater community. I worked with one company that not only had their corporate values well aligned with their corporate strategy and have been achieving great results year over year, but that ensured their values extended well beyond their walls to numerous non-profit organizations and causes at home and abroad.

On one occasion, I had the opportunity to participate in a trip — with a large group of employees from the company — to a children's group home. We had a task list waiting for us upon arrival and I found myself on the crew assigned to helping lay rebar and stone in the basement of a new building being constructed. The concrete was coming in a few days and this foundational work had to get done. When you don't do this kind of labor on a regular basis, it doesn't take long for the aches and pains to set in, but it was all for a good cause.

What really stood out with this company was the C-Suite's commitment to *all* employees. The company had several causes they stood by and supported on a regular basis, and they also considered the causes employees personally cared about and were involved in. Any employee could submit a request for a contribution to their cause. What an incredible way to say, "We care about what you care about too."

I witnessed a high level of morale in this company and I truly believe it was the company's commitment to a strong set of core values, with consistently demonstrated behaviors, that stood as their bedrock of success. I like to think of it as honor on display.

Values in Action

Speaking of "on display," you may or may not see a set of written core values on display in your company. Either way, remember that it's behaviors — not a plaque on the wall — that identify what our values really are. And over time, as you add up everyone's behaviors, you'll have identified the true culture of the organization.

Creating a company strategy steeped in a rich set of core values, exemplified by leadership at all levels, requires commitment, dedication, and a can-do attitude across the board. Teetering back and forth, having one foot in and one foot out, or however you want to say it, won't get it done. Be better, know better, and DO better.

Creating a company strategy steeped in a rich set of core values, exemplified by leadership at all levels, requires commitment, dedication, and a can-do attitude across the board.

A Recommendation: Conduct a Personal SWOT Analysis

I have found it to be very valuable in Corporate America to apply my own personal SWOT analysis for the environment in which I find myself (I know, I know, I sound like an MBA student, but this is a tool that anyone and everyone can use to sharpen their leadership!). I assess my strength and weaknesses (internal forces), opportunities and threats (external forces), based on my own observations and research. It can be valuable to do this while you're going through the hiring process for a new job, and you can get your data by talking with others, searching available information on the company, and asking thought-provoking questions during interviews. At this juncture, if a job is offered and accepted, the SWOT you created becomes a living, transparent analysis that you can share with your team and your boss (and, yes, I really do this). It serves as an input for defining objectives and the desired key results achieved when the objectives are met. It also serves as an alignment tool between personal, department, and corporate strategy.

PERSONAL SWOT ANALYSIS

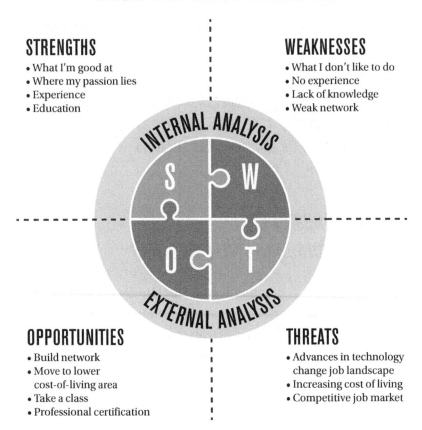

STRENGTHS
- What I'm good at
- Where my passion lies
- Experience
- Education

WEAKNESSES
- What I don't like to do
- No experience
- Lack of knowledge
- Weak network

OPPORTUNITIES
- Build network
- Move to lower cost-of-living area
- Take a class
- Professional certification

THREATS
- Advances in technology change job landscape
- Increasing cost of living
- Competitive job market

Now what do you do with it? Develop a strategy based on a combination of an internal bullet item with an external one. Example:

- **(W)eakness** – Lack of Knowledge
- **(O)pportunity** – Take a Class/Seminar

This represents a WO strategy wherein you then go to work finding the right class at the right institution to give you the knowledge you need to turn it in to a strength. This is a simple illustration of using a tool to move you from "where do I start" to execution. Apply it personally and in the workplace.

CHAPTER 8

The Will to Change and Act

Insights from Dan Denison, Global Consultant, Author, and Management School Professor

Daniel (Dan) Denison is a global consultant, business founder and leader, author, professor, and just a down-right humble and kind human being. I had the honor of first meeting Dan through a grad school classmate who worked for Dan's company, Denison Consulting. Not too long thereafter, I purchased and read Dan's 2012 book, *Leading Culture Change in Global Organizations: Aligning Culture and Strategy*. The book, which Dan co-authored with Robert Hooijberg, Nancy Lane, and Colleen Lief, piqued my interests immediately. I knew right away I wanted to talk to Dan about my book project.

So he and I met, we talked, we broke bread together, and he made me laugh. I asked Dan if it was okay to publish the joke he told me and he kindly agreed with a smile. So here it is:

> *"How many consultants does it take to change a lightbulb?*
>
> *Just one, but the lightbulb has to WANT to change!"*

I laughed because it's so incredibly true. Leaders rarely change if they don't want to. Companies hire consultants all the time and expect to get miraculous results or be presented with a game-changing idea because somehow the consulting firm has a crystal ball with all the answers. Sometimes we experience a leader who's just like the lightbulb, an inanimate object or a "stuck in a rut" leader who does nothing unless something or someone flips his switch and he wants to make a change. For greatness to emerge — in careers and in organizations — it's paramount that we first move from the depth of darkness to the brightness of light, wherein the want and desire to change is discovered. Without doing so, it doesn't matter what the consultant presents or how many of them present it. It goes nowhere and it gets there fast.

Dan's consulting company, headquartered in Ann Arbor, Michigan, competes with the big firms like McKinsey, Deloitte, and others. The evening after I met with Dan, he was heading to Saudi Arabia to kick off a consulting job with the country's largest telecom company, a partnership for which he and his team worked hard to win. Aside from Dan's notable resume full of accomplishments, it's the following quote from Dan's book that I homed in on right away:

> *"**Behavior** must be rooted in a set of core values, and people must be skilled at putting these values into action by reaching agreement while incorporating diverse points of view. These organizations have highly committed employees, a distinct method of doing business, a tendency to promote from within, and a clear set of do's and don'ts."*

I highlighted the word "behavior" because it's the absolute most important point I wanted to make in my own book. It's the very first part of my formula in Chapter 1. Behaviors are the sum total of actions taken by an organization's people and make the difference between good and bad company cultures, business prowess and business weakness, as well as winners and losers.

Behaviors are the sum total of actions taken by an organization's people and make the difference between good and bad company cultures, business prowess and business weakness, as well as winners and losers.

Dan and I also discussed leadership. While I didn't share the details of my previous conversations with the other leaders profiled in this book (i.e., Mike and Rachel), Dan's experience and feedback on this topic was well aligned with theirs and mine. It's what prompted the lightbulb joke. Leadership often can't get out of its own way and there's intense fear of making the wrong decision, so either no decision is made, or one is made that's safe and less risky, but produces lackluster results. But when leaders have the personal courage to take the right risks, remarkable things can happen. Dan's book is chock-full of case studies and examples of companies that have tackled "culture dilemmas" and mastered key culture dynamics to become and remain competitive.

CHAPTER 9
The Facts
Leadership, by the Numbers

Values matter, and behaving in accordance with shared values can generate powerful organizational results. I know it in my bones and I've seen it demonstrated time and again throughout my career. Before you picked up this book, maybe you hadn't given it a whole lot of thought, but I'm guessing you can now think back to all the good things that happened in organizations where leaders and employees were acting in alignment with core values ... and to all the unfortunate or even disastrous things that happened when people behaved in ways completely unguided by shared values.

Values matter, and behaving in accordance with shared values can generate powerful organizational results.

As for the fact that values matter, don't just take my word for it. A 2018 Gallup study[1] argued that "A values-driven culture can fuel organizational growth and attract top talent. Talented people want to work for an organization with a thriving culture." But, sadly, that same study revealed that only 27% of employees strongly agree that they believe

---

1   https://www.gallup.com/workplace/243434/time-core-values-audit.aspx

in their company's values and just 23% strongly agree that they can apply their organization's value to their everyday work.

My own research (among United States workers, aged 25-65, with individual incomes ranging from $75,000 to $200,000), supports these discouraging statistics. Rather than ask the more than 100 participants from my own research study whether they believed in their company's values and could apply them to their work (as Gallup did in their research), I started at a more foundation level, seeking to understand **whether people know if their companies even have stated core values**, and then asking whether their supervisor's behaviors matched those core values.

The majority of respondents to my survey indicated that their company has some set of stated "core values," but 25% indicated that their companies don't have established core values at all, or that the use or application or understanding of them is pretty weak.

Twenty-five percent of survey respondents indicated that their companies don't have established core values at all, or that the use or application or understanding of them is pretty weak.

How would you answer the question "My company has established core values" if allowed to answer on a scale ranging from "strongly disagree" to "strongly agree?" Are they on your website and on your walls? Can you rattle them off without looking? Have you made a decision in your work this week or recently that was specifically guided by your allegiance to those values?

In my research, I gathered data from more than 100 participants. But imagine if the 25% statistic could be extrapolated to 1,000 companies. It's hard not to gulp in fear when imagining that 250 of those companies would have no established values, or poorly articulated and activated ones, at best! Sounds crazy, but believable at the same time. Would you not ask those company leadership teams what they base their foundations on? What drives their vision and mission? What do they use to determine the type of talent they want in the company? How do they measure performance? How do they ensure they build a great company culture? How do they know what behavior they want to see, day in and day out, if they don't have values with which to align that behavior?

Think about it in this way too. For those who indicated on my survey that their company has no established core values, it may also suggest that their company leaders have no self-awareness and are simply behaving how they see fit ... without evaluating how others see their behaviors. That could be ego getting in the way, over confidence but *under* competence, or maybe even being overwhelmed by daily activities they don't take time to pause and assess.

I went on to ask the survey participants **whether their supervisor's behavior matches the company's core values**. A whopping 32% of participants answered in the negative. This is not surprising, as leadership gaps are a real issue that organizations deal with. The military, the government, our non-profit, and our for-profit sectors all need outstanding leadership to thrive.

The key is in how an organization responds to the gap. If this survey was specific to a single organization, we could garner additional, rich insights that would help drive the plan of action to fill the gap. Sounds simple enough, but we must be mindful of the fact that this hypothetical organization is operating with a third of its supervisors not aligned with the organization's core values. Imagine a 10,000-employee, nationwide company wherein 3,200 of those employees don't believe their supervisor's behavior is aligned with the company's core values. Where does leadership begin if they truly wanted this to change? Where would *you* begin? Training

and development, establish and implement a continuous communications plan, and follow-up, follow-up, follow-up are just a few
thoughts that come to mind.

*Imagine a 10,000-employee, nationwide company wherein 3,200
of those employees don't believe their supervisor's behavior is
aligned with the company's core values. Where does leadership
begin if they truly wanted this to change? Where would you begin?*

TIP

Whether your company has 10 employees or 10,000
employees, conduct an anonymous employee survey about
values, behavior, and leadership. Find out whether your
employees know the values your founders have established
and evolved over the years. Determine whether they believe
in them and strive to behave in accordance with them.
Discover whether you have divisions or leadership levels
where values-based behavior is stellar and other areas where
aligning behavior to values could be improved. Get the
facts, and then get busy making your organization better.

On this survey, I asked two more questions. The first was **whether
participants support their company's core values**. The good news
was that most respondents agreed that they do, in fact, support the
core values espoused by their employer. But 27% don't care or are
not aligned with their company's core values. It would be fascinating
to dive deeper into this group with onsite types of studies to see if
"support" equals "behaviors" we could define as aligned with core
values. I also can't help but wonder what the employee turnover

looks like in companies like this, whether they're meeting sales/ revenue targets, and how they're doing in terms of profitability margins or fundraising goals.

In a large organization, these 27% — the people who don't care about the core values and might even be working in opposition to them — may be able to skate by and hide behind others. In small organizations, they're toxic to the workplace environment and have the potential to create drama, rumor mills, and do about anything other than being productive.

On this survey, my final question was about the highest levels of leadership, asking respondents to indicate **whether they believe their company's leadership lives by the core values**. Respondents overwhelming agreed (63%) that their organization's top leaders are practicing what they preach. They're not the "do as I say, not as I do" type of people. There were 19% of the survey participants who *strongly* agree that their leaders live by the core values; these respondents may be identifying the type of leader who not only practices what they preach, but also says "here, let me show you how it's done" and rolls up their sleeves and joins their teams side-by-side ... not to brag or watch, but to teach, guide, and mentor.

Now what about the 37% who don't believe their company's leadership live by the core values? Can you identify with them because you've experienced people in leadership positions like that? These *are* the "do as I say, not as I do" people. Or they could simply be the people who have never had the opportunity to participate in a formal leadership and development (L&D) program. How many of those even exist in companies these days, now that bosses are apt to think you can get all your learning from a Google search or a $79 webinar? While I was perhaps not as grateful as I could have been when going through all the leadership training I had during my 26+ years in the Army. I'm surely grateful for it now. While it disheartens me to think about the organizations being led by leaders who don't behave in accordance with admirable core values, I'm hesitant to point fingers or criticize too harshly. Because I know that people are often put into leadership positions having had zero training and development, so they simply have to wing it.

What Values Are YOU Guided By?

Throughout this book, I've talked a great deal about values and why they matter, how they must be demonstrated through day-to-day behavior, and how they are the bedrock for organizational cultures. I've shared the values that guide *me* (i.e., the Army values of Loyalty, Duty, Respect, Selfless Service, Honor, Integrity, and Personal Courage). And I shared the values that drive organizations like JetBlue. Ever curious, I wanted to know what other people considered to be the most important values in the American workplace. So I conducted yet another survey.

Respondents were aged 25 to 65, a nearly even male/female split, with annual individual incomes ranging from $75,000 to $200,000. In this survey, I asked people to tell me **what their top 3 most important values were for the workplace**. I then took all their responses and put them in to a word cloud (in case you didn't know, Microsoft PowerPoint has a word cloud add-in — no other software needed). This is something you can easily do in your own organization too. It's a great collaboration and inclusion exercise to keep in your toolkit. But here's a tip ... don't do this in the workplace only to turnaround and create new core values that are *not* aligned with people's responses found in the word cloud. If you do that, you've just single-handedly demonstrated you couldn't care less about what others think. Use this tool with the right intent and commitment. It'll show employees their voices are being heard.

What you find in your organization might be fascinating and even game-changing. Here's what I found on my marketplace survey ...

The Survey Word Cloud

If you've never seen a word cloud before (or never been aware of the rhyme and reason behind the sizes of the words), here's the scoop. The larger a word appears in the cloud, the more frequently it was mentioned in the survey answers. It's a tremendous visualization to demonstrate what values people find most important. It doesn't mean that a smaller, less-represented word is insignificant; every bit of feedback from stakeholders is worthy of our consideration. Here is the word cloud generated from the survey I conducted:

I absolutely love this visual response! Imagine that — honesty and integrity come out on top. Whether or not those two values are written in your company's core values, do you witness them in your

---

2   https://hbr.org/2016/10/why-leadership-training-fails-and-what-to-do-about-it

workplace? When using this tool to help define core values, take the words and do the following:

- Write out their full dictionary definitions, including any noun or verb variations
- Read the definitions you just wrote down
- Brainstorm which verbs (action words) bring the word cloud words to life (like "tell the truth" for the value of honesty) and list them separately
- Write out the full definition of each of the verbs on the list
- Write out people behaviors that would align with those definitions
- Formulate a story of how a person should then behave in your workplace
- Start with your team and study whether their behaviors match the story
- Find the gaps, make a plan to fill the gaps, and execute it

The Exercise in Action: Honesty

Following the first six steps above, this is what honesty in the workplace would look like:

1. Definition (dictionary.com) – noun, plural hon·es·ties.
   - the quality or fact of being honest; uprightness and fairness
   - truthfulness, sincerity, or frankness
   - freedom from deceit or fraud

2. Verbs to demonstrate honesty
   - **tell** the truth
   - **express** sincerity
   - **reject** fraudulent behaviors
   - **treat** ALL team members fairly

3. Verb definitions (dictionary.com)
   - Tell – to give an account or narrative of; narrate; relate (a story, tale, etc.); to make known by speech or writing (a fact, news, information, etc.); communicate
   - Express – (used with object) to put (thought) into words; utter or state; to express an idea clearly; to show, manifest, or reveal; to express one's anger
   - Reject – to refuse to have, take, recognize, etc.; to reject the offer of a better job; to refuse to grant (a request, demand, etc.); to refuse to accept (someone or something); rebuff
   - Treat – to act or behave toward (a person) in some specified way; to consider or regard in a specified way, and deal with accordingly

4. People behaviors in the workplace associated with the verbs listed above may include items such as the following:
   - Email that focuses on the facts, not the rumor mill, and gets to the point with politicizing or getting personal
   - Shut down the rumor mill using appropriate words regarding those engaged in it
   - Open the door for others; shake a team member's hand or give a high-five for a job well done
   - Work through issues until you have a solution that creates the opportunity for a win-win-win outcome (employee wins, team wins, company wins)

5. The story – "All of our team members at ABC Company are critical to the company achieving its mission. We believe in treating everyone with dignity and respect and presenting the truth in all we do. From an open-door policy to team collaboration to generating the best possible practices and solutions for our employees and clients alike, ABC Company stands on its core values above all else. Never jeopardize your honor. Instead, live by it alongside us and we'll soar to new heights together."

In relatively short order, we have a one-pager on the value of "Honesty" in the workplace.

Do Employees Have a Voice When It Comes to Values?

I asked one more question of the respondents to my second survey ... I wanted to know **whether they believed that their company or organization leadership would take their values feedback seriously.**

It's important to know whether employees feel like their leadership "listens" to their feedback. I coach leaders regularly on the importance of having a plan of action in place to respond to employee feedback in a purposeful way. If not planning to respond with purpose, even in the cases of not liking the feedback, *not* responding is worse than having not sought out the feedback in the first place. Make the intent of seeking employee feedback well known and communicate it according to a clear and concise communications plan. Project managers know this method well and all good PMs have the communications plan outlined in their project plans.

Make the intent of seeking employee feedback well known and communicate it according to a clear and concise communications plan.

In the responses to this question, participants were relatively in line with the results of my first. About 30% gave a neutral response (perhaps indicative of the fact that they haven't even or wouldn't ever provide feedback to their leadership about values) and 22% indicated that they don't believe their leadership would give serious consideration to their feedback about workplace values.

I ponder all the possible reasons people in leadership positions would not take employee feedback seriously. I'm sure you can imagine a list such as this one:

- I'm in charge and know best
- I have more experience
- I'm smarter than you
- I'm too busy to listen
- We don't have time for this
- Just do what I say
- Do your job and I'll do mine
- I really don't care what you think
- This is what we do, so do it

That list could go on and on. Also think about it from an organizational perspective. Sometimes it's not the leader's fault. They simply have no idea how to respond or behave as a leader. How many organizations today have internal leadership development programs in place or outsource it to consulting companies? Turns out, this is a $160 billion industry in the U.S. that's failing. *Harvard Business Review* does a great job telling us why (be sure to check out the article); as you read it, you'll be able to associate these failures with the poor leadership reasons listed above.[3] People get put into positions of supervising others simply because someone must do it, but what resources has the organization provided them to truly be successful as a leader? Let me be clear, though ... I'm not defending poor leaders because, with or without ample training, there are always those leaders who simply have a terrible outlook, personality, character, etc. and regardless of any leadership training just don't have what it takes. On the other hand, there are fortunately

---

3   https://hbr.org/2016/10/why-leadership-training-fails-and-what-to-do-about-it

many others who have the potential to deliver great leadership and just need investment in their development.

Do you recall from Mike Barger's experience at JetBlue, the crew-member that gets told "you're now the supervisor" and is suddenly in charge of other crewmembers who were his peers the day before? He had no idea how to respond to the single mom employee who had daycare challenges, wherein the daycare opened at the same time her shift was supposed to start. While this might be something a developed, experienced leader who cares about their people would have no issue dealing with, is a BIG problem for the new crew-member in charge. Take a moment and think about how the simple challenges in life for one can be monumental challenges for others. Though all deserve to be treated fairly, with dignity and respect, we're not all equal in our leadership abilities!

CHAPTER 10

The How

Separating the Talkers from the Doers

The "How" is the most essential part of separating the talkers from the doers. You can read book after book about leadership, values, business case studies, personal growth, and on and on. But none of what you read is worth anything (including this book) if YOU don't DO something with what you read. Make a goal to take at least one thing from each professional book you read, put it in your toolkit, and implement it. Do this consistently over time and it will unquestionably take you, your team, and your company to another level. Why? Simply because so many people don't.

Make a goal to take at least one thing from each professional book you read, put it in your toolkit, and implement it. Do this consistently over time and it will unquestionably take you, your team, and your company to another level.

Along with learning from the behaviors on display in the numerous stories throughout this book, I've outlined below some tips and tools in reference to one very essential component of the workplace (i.e., respect) and one key component discussed early on (i.e., paralyzing fear). Both represent considerable forces at play every day in companies across the globe. Let's see what we can do about it.

Respect

In 2018, I co-authored the HR anthology *You@Work: Unlocking Human Potential in the Workplace.* My contribution to the book focused entirely on how to demonstrate respect in the workplace. I've included it here with further re-vision. I truly believe respect is the first cousin of love. Love without action is not love at all and so it goes with respect. If you look up the word respect on dictionary. com, you'll find seven definitions listed as a noun and four listed as a verb. As with any core value we wish to align behaviors with, we must dump the nouns! Behaviors are what matter. You may say words matter too, and I believe that's true as well. We use them to communicate every day, but words without action are just that ... words.

As with any core value we wish to align behaviors with, we must dump the nouns! Behaviors are what matter.

I've designed the model below to provide an insight on how to demonstrate respect. The model is designed to invoke ACTION. It's short, concise and in-your-face — like a Drill Sergeant — so you'll remember: Respect is a verb. It applies to everyone on the team, including the C-suite. As you read through, think of the model as a toolset you can employ during your day. The more complicated a toolset is, the less likely we may be to use it, so here it's simple. As you read through my examples, you'll quickly think of your own that, when added together, will give you plenty of behaviors to look for, push for, cheer for.

The Brabo Model of Respect

- SHOW UP
- SIT UP
- STAND UP
- SPEAK UP
- SHUT UP

Show Up!

If we were to define this in just three words, they'd be "Be on Time." But it's much more than that. Show Up means to be there in the good times and the bad; to bring your A-game every time; to be on time with your work deliverables; to be prepared and on time for meetings; and to be focused on the topic at hand.

Consider an example of a meeting that YOU scheduled with your team. You show up 10 minutes late, have no agenda put together, nothing to present, and you didn't communicate the desired goal/outcome of the meeting. Did you demonstrate any respect for your team? Of course not. In fact, your team members probably left the meeting whispering under their breath or texting each other, saying that was a complete waste of their time (and probably a few other observations, complete with expletives).

With the ever-popular webinar these days, here's another example that I'm sure we've all experienced and, in my humble opinion, it's become commonplace. Regardless of the number of participants that registered for the webinar (really this could be any teleconference or video conference), the organizer welcomes people to the webinar at the scheduled start time and then immediately follows by saying something like, "Let's wait a few minutes as others are still joining the meeting." WHAT??? I showed up on time and now we're waiting! C'mon, I have things to do so let's get this show on the road. Those are my sentiments every time. What's happening in this scenario is the organizer showing respect to those who are late and not respecting the time wasted for those who were on time (aka ... SHOWED UP). In the case of the online meeting or teleconference, the script has flipped, and we need to right the ship.

Take the meeting set-up rules by Jeff Bezos, CEO of Amazon, as an example. Bezos is reported to always ensure an agenda for the meeting is sent to participants in advance, as well as agreeing upon the meeting's desired outcomes before the meeting. Then, when the meeting starts, there is a 10 to 15-minute period of silence for participants to read the agenda and the memo that outlines what's to be discussed during the meeting. In case a participant wasn't prepared, Bezos helps them out just a bit in this way to get them ready for discussion. It's a leadership tactic that highlights the "Show Up" nature of respect.

Sit Up!

This is as much about perception as it is about real respect. Envision a meeting with participants seated around a conference room table or even co-workers at their desks. Are they slouches or sliders (you know the folks ... slid way down in their chairs)? What thoughts come to mind when you see this?

- Not interested
- Lazy
- Mind is elsewhere
- Not getting their work done
- Not taken seriously
- Don't care

- Tired
- Rude
- Etc.

We may have other thoughts as well, but we'll keep those to ourselves. The point here is to be objective about viewing yourself and consider whether this is you or not. If it is, do something about it. We're always being observed by our co-workers (subordinates, peers, and superiors alike) and perception is reality in many cases. It must be addressed and resolved. How do you fix it?

- Sit up in your chair.
- Find a chair that fits you (ergonomics matter).
- Practice good posture.
- In meetings, make eye contact with the person speaking (and this is easier to do when you're sitting up).

A few simple changes and you'll find perception changes at the same time. Now you're a contender; you're present and accounted for; in-turn, while you listen, others will listen to you; you're focused; you're showing respect.

Stand Up!

There are multiple scenarios that occur during the workday where this tool has the potential to elevate you to a different level. First, Stand Up means just that, STAND UP. A physical movement of getting up off your chair and standing on your feet. Consider the following and how another person might truly feel you showed them respect with one quick move:

You are sitting at your desk in your office or at your cubicle, and your boss comes to you to ask a question or give some feedback. At the very moment you know he's there, stand and give him your attention. This will demonstrate your focus and recognition of his authority. The boss will remember you for the respect you showed him. Do it regularly and the boss will know that respect is part of your character. Please take note: This doesn't have to be a scenario with your boss; it can be applied to anyone.

Now, let's say you are the person who stands, and you want to get others to show the same respect. Here's a tip to invoke change on the down-low, because this change is all about behavior and having co-workers follow your lead. When you arrive at a meeting, DO NOT sit down at the table until the leader of the meeting shows up and sits down. Over time, others will start to see what you're doing and may ask you why, thus giving you an opening to explain, or they may simply follow suit. There are more followers in the world than there are leaders and leading doesn't mean having direct reports is a requirement. The best leaders can lead up, down, and sideways (i.e., among superiors, subordinates, and peers), both internal and external to their organizations. Worse case, because you're the one standing and no one else is, your respect for the one leading the meeting will surely be recognized by the leader himself.

There are more followers in the world than there are leaders, and leading doesn't mean having direct reports is a requirement. The best leaders can lead up, down, and sideways.

Speak Up!

Of the five points in the model, this may be the one that's not the easiest to accomplish, especially if you're an introvert and only think of it as verbal speaking in front of others. At work, at home, and in life,

YOU are unique and have ideas, thoughts and feelings — important things that others should hear ... or READ. But you must share them.

Let's talk about sharing these important things in a respectful manner. I've used the meeting set-up in previous examples, so I'll build upon that here too. Regardless of the type of meeting (e.g., in-person, teleconference, webinar, etc.), there is a time for each participant to speak. Keeping that in mind, we need to take a step back for just a moment. Meetings have topics or reasons for occurring. Preparation for the meeting is the key to speaking in the meeting. You must take the time to prepare before attending the meeting and make pre-meeting notes (comments and questions) before ever stepping foot in the meeting or joining the call. If you happen to be the introvert, this alone will help you gain the confidence to Speak Up during the meeting itself.

Speak Up also has another connotation regarding others showing YOU respect. For those of you responsible for leading others, do you have their back? Do you *really* have their back? Do you Speak Up on their behalf, or are you the one who takes credit for their work when it's good but throws them under the bus when it's bad? If you're "that person," you're not a leader at all and will never earn their respect. I don't say this here to sound tough, but to invoke self-reflection and to ensure that, if nothing else, anyone in a leadership position reading this understands that those they lead deserve their voice on their behalf. Speak Up, give credit, and take the heat!

Let me share a quick story about speaking up. There are plenty of movies and TV shows with bar scenes, wherein the bartender is giving counsel to one of the main characters of the show. The bartender, having had numerous conversations with customers, has amassed the wisdom of a profound psychologist. The same holds true for barbers in a barbershop. Not long ago, while I was getting a haircut, my barber, Nick, and I talked a lot about football — because it was football season and there was much to talk about. Aside from discussing who was winning, losing, getting suspended, or paying fines, Nick told me about his son, who played quarterback on his high school football team. One key piece of advice he gave his son, which I took from our conversation, was that his job as the quarterback was to lead his team and get the ball into the hands of the playmakers.

Pause and think about the last sentence. Nick also explained that often when we see the quarterback double-clutch before throwing, it's because the receiver wasn't where he was supposed to be according to the play the quarterback called in the huddle. The quarterback must adjust, therefore we the fans see the double-clutch. When the game is over and the quarterback is answering questions during the post-game press conference, it's inevitable that a reporter asks, "Did you lose the game due to all the double-clutching in the pocket? Why did you pause so much on throwing the ball?" And here's where it gets real and Nick's barbershop counsel is on-point. The quarterback leader's response is, "We didn't play as well as we did in practice and I should have been better at calling the right plays." Whoa!! Nick you are brilliant. The quarterback who respects his teammates does not tell the reporter it's because the receiver didn't memorize the playbook and kept running the wrong routes. He takes the heat. He speaks up on behalf of his entire team. That's showing respect.

Shut Up!

Harsh? I hope so. Just as there's a time to speak, there's also a time to keep your lips in contact with one another. If you've been part of any group meeting, I'd find it hard to believe that you have never witnessed people speaking, whispering, gossiping, interrupting or committing a slew of other offenses when someone else had the floor. Repetitive behavior like this is *dis*-respect deserving of being called out as it's happening. To be clear and non-politically correct, Shut Up really does mean Shut Up.

Just as we need to know when to speak up, we need to also recognize when it's time to not speak (more politically correct maybe). Here's a short list of those times:

- Anytime someone else is speaking (or "has the floor," so to say)
- When your comment has nothing to do with the topic
- When all you have is a joke (it may not be funny or appropriate to all)
- When you're speaking just to hear yourself speak (demonstrating arrogance versus respect).

Have you ever been somewhere, say a restaurant or a movie theater, when someone's phone rings and then they sit right there and take the call? I imagine that you have had this experience, as I have, and it tends to stir up a lot of emotions (not the good ones). The person taking the call is showing their narcissistic, disrespectful self to the world around them. What about a similar scenario during a meeting at work? The person who did that at the restaurant will do it in the meeting too. The solution may be obvious to most but needs to be said anyway: If your phone must be on during a meeting and then a call comes in (hopefully it's on vibrate or silent), you have two choices to show respect to those around you: 1) Let the call go to voicemail and deal with it later, or 2) Pick up your phone, leave the meeting and take the call in private elsewhere. Others in the meeting will see your respect and appreciate your actions.

Sidebar conversations are another example of disrespecting the speaker, and it happens regularly. The disruption or annoyance for those hearing the sidebar, even for the speaker, is much like the heckler to a comedian on stage. It throws off concentration and focus and has the potential to derail the entire flow of the meeting. What to do? If you're the sidebar talker (or heckler, as I'll call you), you need to learn how to zip it; if what you have to say is relevant, share it with the group when it's your time to speak. If it's super important at that moment, take a play from the schoolhouse classroom and raise your hand ... that, folks, is showing respect.

I've witnessed the good, the bad and the ugly when it comes to demonstrating respect. Through our actions, we are fully capable of generating feelings, emotions and even modeling good behavior in others. As previously stated, respect, much like love, is empty without the right behaviors to back it up. If we all did our best to employ this model and show respect to others as a regular part of our lives, we would change the world ... one respectful action at a time!

One quick story on respect in action. My wife and I recently had the opportunity to have breakfast with Dymonte Thomas. Dymonte is a University of Michigan grad and, at the time of our breakfast, an NFL player with the Denver Broncos. We met this young man through my Michigan grad school classmate, Vince Calo (attorney and NFL agent). The four of us sat at The Mocha House in Warren, Ohio, and talked for a few hours about real estate investing and, most of all, transitioning to a second career. My wife and I arrived first, each grabbed a cup of coffee and chose a table that offered us some privacy. While waiting, I saw Dymonte coming up the stairs toward the entrance doors and then he stopped. Behind him were two elderly ladies and he waited for them so he could open and hold the rather heavy entrance doors for them. Small act of respect, big display of his kindness and character!

Fear and Worry

In the interviews I conducted with Rachel Noble and Dan Denison for this book, much was said about fear and how paralyzing it can be.

Fear can keep us from reaching our true potential. It holds people back from taking the risk that needs to be taken to rise above the rest — to be the industry leader, to maximize sales and profits. If this is you, even just sometimes, what can you do about it? From me to you, here's an exercise you can use to face fear head-on and, over time, overcome it with regularity.

1. Write things down. Take what's in your head and put it on paper; use real pen to paper or type in a Word document. List all the negative outcomes that you can think of if you made the decision or took the action that you're too afraid to make or take.

2. Each of those items now becomes an item to address individually. Now rank them from 1 to 10, with 1 being those of minimal risk and 10 being those of extreme risk. Remember, this is YOUR exercise and assessment, so be brutally honest with yourself.

3. Put all the numbers, 1 through 10, and create sublists — one list for items you gave a 10, another list for items you gave a 9, etc.

4. Start with the 1s and write down all the things you could do to overcome that negative outcome and what the positive outcome would be if you did it. Start writing all those positive outcomes on a separate list. Move on to the 2s and so on, until you finish with the 10s.

5. Time to be vulnerable. Take your work from above and share it with your closest confidant, mentor, pastor, priest, friend, colleague, or mental health professional and talk through them. You must verbalize the words in this step with another person, drawing attention to your list of positive outcomes.

6. After this conversation, or multiple conversations, update your list of positive outcomes.

7. Read this new list to yourself day-in and day-out until acting

on them becomes simple to do and the fear of doing so is no longer there.

When we write and talk, we can get things off our minds. We can get out of our own way. I often counsel employees by simply starting with "Go ahead, get it off your mind" or "Tell me all about it." I avoid questions, which — for people under duress — can feel like an inquisition. Instead, I make welcoming statements that lead to free-flowing thoughts getting out. Typical responses I get in return after such a conversation? "That was a relief." ... "Glad I got that out" ... "Thank you for listening."

I often counsel employees by simply starting with "Go ahead, get it off your mind" or "Tell me all about it." I avoid questions, which — for people under duress — can feel like an inquisition.

One's faith can also have a powerful impact on their ability to overcome fear. For me personally, I had an epiphany about five years ago and it had a deep impact on eliminating fear and worry from my life. It was a Sunday morning and I was sitting in church. It was one of the Sundays I feel blessed to not have missed. The youth pastor had the stage and after he made announcements from the bulletin, he asked the congregation a question and he wanted people to raise their hands and give an answer. He asked, "What command from God is said the most times in the Bible?" Several hands went up immediately and he called on a few to give their answers. One person said "To love each other," another said "To preach the Gospel," and yet another chimed in with "To treat others as you want to be treated." The youth pastor replied with a "Nope. Those are all good answers, but they aren't it. The answer is to *not fear or worry*." 360+ plus times throughout the Bible, God says do not fear, do not worry.

For I am the Lord your God who takes hold of your right hand and says to you, do not fear; I will help you … - Isaiah 41:13

On that Sunday, I realized that, if I was a man of faith, I really needed to start listening and that day was as good a time as any to do so. The bondage of fear and worry was broken!

"Courage to Change the Things I Can"

American theologian Reinhold Niebuhr wrote what has become known far and wide as The Serenity Prayer. It goes like this: "God, grant me the serenity to accept the things I cannot change, Courage to change the things I can, And wisdom to know the difference." And it's stitched on a lot of pillows and hanging on a lot of dining room walls. That "wisdom to know the difference" is about understanding what you can control.

Fear and worry — at work and at home — can be addressed through an understanding of control. Go back to the pen and paper and list out all the things you can personally control. Not the things you can have an impact upon, but those you can actually control.

Examples of what I can control:

- What time I set my alarm for
- What I chose to eat
- How I respond when someone is talking to me
- How fast or slow I drive my car
- Whether or not I open the door for my wife
- How much I tip at a restaurant
- The level of effort I put in on the job
- How many books I read
- How many words I write

- How I treat people at home, at work, at the grocery store, and everywhere I go.

Examples of what I *can't* control:
- The electricity going out during the middle of the night
- The weather
- How others treat me or what they think of me
- How slow or fast others are driving
- When the department of transportation decides to do road work
- Who runs for President or who wins
- What time the mail gets delivered
- The price of a new iPhone
- How fresh the produce is at the time I buy it
- My daughter's school grades

These lists could each have hundreds of items. Regardless of the number of examples on your lists, pay attention to the ones you put on the control list. This is where your power lies. Next step? Take time to write out the *behaviors* you'd have to exude in order to put that power to work FOR YOU. In essence, you're taking ownership and authority over what you can control and not worrying about what you can't control.

Imagine you're on a business development team and you have to prepare a proposed acquisition pipeline. You want the company to expand into a new region overseas. You've identified a path to incredible returns for the company, but it requires a level of risk the company has not taken in the past. You've also witnessed leadership in the past respond harshly to risky plans. But there's a new VP at the helm of business development, as well as a new CEO. You are petrified they'll think your expansion plan is ill-fated and you'll get your head ripped off (figuratively). Plus, you're known to not take criticism well, so what will you do?

What can you control in this scenario? Several things. You control what details get included in the proposal (e.g., financial projections, foreign government rules/pitfalls/benefits, growth projections). You control the degree to which you are prepared for the pitch. You control whether you take time in advance to prepare thoughtful responses to anticipated questions and concerns. You control whether you go into the room with an alternative course of action or a Plan B.

What can you NOT control? A few things. You can't control their responses, their questions, their concerns, or their final decision.

Bottom line: Act on what you CAN control. You'll see that even in scenarios like this, it may just outweigh what you CAN'T control, and you'll be off to the races!

CHAPTER 11

The Army Values

Admirable Guideposts for Wherever You Lead

This is my salute to the core values of the United States Army. In some ways, this entire book has been a salute to those value, which are tried and true. These seven values have been tested by tens of thousands with their blood, sweat, and tears. They've been lived up to by millions more.

If you're struggling in your own organization to determine what your core values should be, emulate these (some or all) and you can't go wrong. Build from there, and find the guideposts that work most powerfully for your organization and its people.

The acronym for the Army values is LDRSHIP (aka ... leadership). They go like this:*

Loyalty

Bear true faith and allegiance to the U.S. Constitution, the Army, your unit and other Soldiers. Bearing true faith and allegiance is a matter of believing in and devoting yourself to something or someone. A loyal Soldier is one who supports the leadership and stands up

---

* Since I was just 17 years old, I've been immersed in the Army values. I've seen them on posters, read them in handbooks, heard them explained by mentors and commanding officers. I could recite them in my sleep and explain them at a moment's notice. Descriptions you'll find from various sources may vary a bit, but the essence is always the same. Learn more at https://www.army.mil/values/.

for fellow Soldiers. By wearing the uniform of the U.S. Army, you are expressing your loyalty. And by doing your share, you show your loyalty to your unit.

Duty

Fulfill your obligations. Doing your duty means more than carrying out your assigned tasks. Duty means being able to accomplish tasks as part of a team. The work of the U.S. Army is a complex combination of missions, tasks, and responsibilities — all in constant motion. Our work entails building one assignment onto another. You fulfill your obligations as a part of your unit every time you resist the temptation to take "shortcuts" that might undermine the integrity of the final product.

Respect

Treat people as they should be treated. In the Soldier's Code, we pledge to "treat others with dignity and respect while expecting others to do the same." Respect is what allows us to appreciate the best in other people. Respect is trusting that all people have done their jobs and fulfilled their duty. And self-respect is a vital ingredient with the Army value of respect, which results from knowing you have put forth your best effort. The Army is one team and each of us has something to contribute.

Selfless Service

Put the welfare of the nation, the Army, and your subordinates before your own. Selfless service is larger than just one person. In serving your country, you are doing your duty loyally without thought of recognition or gain. The basic building block of selfless service is

the commitment of each team member to go a little further, endure
a little longer, and look a little closer to see how he or she can add to
the effort.

Honor

Live up to Army values. The nation's highest military award is The
Medal of Honor. This award goes to Soldiers who make honor
a matter of daily living — Soldiers who develop the habit of being
honorable, and solidify that habit with every value choice they make.
Honor is a matter of carrying out, acting, and living the values of
respect, duty, loyalty, selfless service, integrity, and personal courage
in everything you do.

Integrity

Do what's right, legally and morally. Integrity is a quality you develop
by adhering to moral principles. It requires that you do and say
nothing that deceives others. As your integrity grows, so does the
trust others place in you. The more choices you make based on integrity, the more this highly prized value will affect your relationships
with family and friends, and, finally, the fundamental acceptance
of yourself.

Personal Courage

Face fear, danger or adversity (physical or moral). Personal courage
has long been associated with our Army. With physical courage, it is
a matter of enduring physical duress and at times risking personal
safety. Facing moral fear or adversity may be a long, slow process
of continuing forward on the right path, especially if taking those
actions is not popular with others. You can build your personal

courage by daily standing up for and acting upon the things that you know are honorable.

The Army values written here are done so with purpose. Read them as they are. Read them as a Soldier reads them. They're full of actions you can take now (i.e., the DO). They're full of the types of behavior you can influence others to take — the types of behavior worthy of emulation. In further honor of the Army's leadership mantra ... "Be, Know, Do" ... BE one with the core values, KNOW them inside and out, and DO them without fail.

CHAPTER 12

The Courage to Lead
Taking the Next Step

You made it this far. Now the challenge is to do something with what you learned. Keep this book as a reference when you need it. You have read through it once, and may find value in going back through these pages to re-read the parts that intrigued you the most. Write things down and apply them to your own stories and experiences. Dive in to defining the behaviors that make up your company's core values. If that seems too daunting at first, start with your own personal values. How do you characterize your own behaviors at home, at work, and in the community? It may help to ask your closest family members and friends to tell you stories about times when they saw you at your best. It's called the "Reflective Best Self" exercise. You'll get more than what you expect and most likely you'll be reminded of stories you had all but forgotten — stories that meant something to the storyteller but maybe not to you. This exercise is an opportunity to see yourself through the eyes of others.

Dive in to defining the behaviors that make up your company's core values

Start the conversation at work. Talk to your coworkers about their views of the company's core values. If their views are negative, skeptical, or apathetic, talk about what you can do to change that. How can you be a champion of that change? Choose the leader in the company you think is most well aligned with the core values and go talk to them too. The more positive energy that gets flowing, the better the odds of some real change happening. Keep the momentum going.

I call this PEDL (pronounced pedal). It's an acronym that stands for Participate, Engage, Discuss, and Learn. The analogy is that of pedaling a bicycle. Never stop pedaling to move forward. Keep in mind, you can stop pedaling and coast for a while, but eventually the bike will simply stop, and you'll fall over. The same holds true for change initiatives in the workplace, especially ones that involve aligning the appropriate behaviors with the core values.

I truly hope you enjoyed reading this book, getting to know me, and considering the power you have to inspire positive change. Values-based results are within your reach. I wish you all the success in the world. Go be the kind of leader who does this right. *Hooah!*

ACKNOWLEDGMENTS

I could not have written this book without the loving support of **my wife, Marci, and my daughters Ellen and Clara**. I could not be more blessed than to have your love and support! I do what I do for all of you. We all push hard every day, striving to be better than we were the day before and encourage others along our journey to reach for the stars. The hustle is real and with God guiding our steps, all things are possible.

To **Senior Drill Sergeant Ellis, Drill Sergeant Barefield, and Drill Sergeant Brunais**, my three platoon Drill Sergeants — You were as tough as nails and personally responsible for turning thousands of young men into Soldiers. You exemplified the Army values of Loyalty, Duty, Respect, Selfless Service, Honor, Integrity, and Personal Courage. THANK YOU from the bottom of my heart. You changed my life more than you'll ever know.

Thank you, **Staff Sergeant Byrd**, for all your instruction, counseling, and confidence in your student. I will forever remember what I learned about leadership ... and about myself ... during PLDC.

To **Sergeant Sydney Williams and Specialist Joey Ellington** — Joey E. and Lil'Sip — for singing and entertaining us through the perils of serving in Iraq. The "shower hour" were some of my best memories in the battlefield and I can't thank you enough for using your talents to keep morale high and making the stressors of war a little less each and every day.

To my **White House Communications Agency teammates**. It was a privilege and honor to serve alongside you. Together, we provided the President with the highest quality communications as possible. We did it with no rehearsals, on tight timelines, and always with determination to be the best of the best. We did it as a team, with no one of us less important than the other. You are all forever part of my White House story.

To my amazing book coach, **Cathy Fyock**, for your advice, support, and helping keep me on track. And to my editor and publisher **Kate Colbert**, my publicist **Stephanie Feger**, and the entire team at **Silver Tree Publishing**, thank you for believing in this book (and me!) and helping make this dream a reality. What a phenomenal team!

A very special "thank you" to the contributors of this book who spent hours listening to me, answering my questions, and simply being tremendously kind human beings. **Mike Barger, Rachel Noble, and Dan Denison**, you are the best! Thank you!

A second word of deep gratitude to **Mike Barger** for writing the foreword for this book. I am honored beyond measure.

Thank you to my endorsers — **Colonel Luis A. Parilli, Brent Westhoven, CW2 Bernard Simmons, and Lieutenant Colonel Chris Roth**. Your words humble me.

Last, but not least, a final message of gratitude for my friend Brent. Many of my experiences, stories, and opportunities in life can be linked to a single phone call back in 1997. Then Staff Sergeant **Brent Westhoven** called me and recruited me for a special Army assignment. He said something like, "Would you be interested in a special assignment? We'll send you to Airborne school so you can learn how to jump out of planes." That was about it and I said *yes*! Ever since that moment, Brent has been a best friend, my brother in arms, my confidant, and mentor. We've worked together, started a business together, closed a business together, played a lot of golf, and simply shared the ups and downs of life over the past 23 years and counting. To Brent, thank you for being you!

KEEP IN TOUCH

Learn more about Bo and get a conversation started:

RobertBrabo.com

Send an email:

Bo@RobertBrabo.com

Find, follow, engage, and share on social media:

Twitter.com/Bo_Brabo

LinkedIn.com/in/RobertBrabo

Instagram.com/BoBrabo

Facbook.com/RobertBoBrabo

Listen to The Bo & Luke Show podcast:

HailMediaGroup.com/Bo-and-Luke-Show
and everywhere podcasts are delivered!

ABOUT THE AUTHOR

Throughout his career, Robert "Bo" Brabo has always focused on the people, helping them tackle their challenges as if they were his own. Since retiring from the U.S. Army as the Chief of HR Operations with the White House Communications Agency and as a Presidential Communications Officer for President George W. Bush and President Barack Obama, Bo has served in several executive positions, including most recently as Vice President of Human Resources at the National Spine and Pain Centers and as Principal at HAIL Ventures and Consulting. He also previously co-founded a consulting agency that assisted government contractors in HR strategies and contract proposal efforts.

Bo Brabo is a sought-after professional speaker, leadership consultant, and values-based HR leader. He received his MBA for the University of Michigan's Ross School of Business, is the co-host of The Bo & Luke Show podcast, and is committed to lifelong learning and sharing, to make us all stronger. His insights have appeared in professional journals and in the 2018 HR anthology, *You@Work: Unlocking Human Potential in the Workplace.*

From the Battlefield to the White House to the Boardroom: Leading Organizations to Values-Based Results is his first solo-authored nonfiction business book.

Made in the USA
Monee, IL
03 March 2020

22674205R00095